Modern Architecture in Finland

Asko Salokorpi

Weidenfeld and Nicolson
5 Winsley Street London W1

First published in England in 1970 by
George Weidenfeld and Nicolson Ltd
Text by Asko Salokorpi
Designed by Juha Anttinen
Printed in Denmark by F. E. Bording Limited

Acknowledgments

The author and publishers wish to thank all those listed below
who have kindly supplied photographs for this book:
Stndio Apollo; H. Havas; H. Iffland; P. Ingervo; M. I. Jaatinen;
J. Könönen; O. Laiho; E. Mäkinen; R. Paatelainen; J. Pallasmaa;
Studio Pietinen; S. Rista; Studio Roos; M. Saanlo; A. Salokorpi;
G. Welin; N. E. Wickberg.

Cover illustration: The students union building (Dipoli)
at Otaniemi, by Reima Pietilä
and Raili Paatelainen (1966).

Modern Architecture in Finland

Introduction

It is understood nowadays that architecture is total environment and that buildings are only a part of this environment.

In classical town planning buildings were the dominant factor; they formed groups and enclosed spaces. Since the Renaissance the planting of trees and shrubs and the laying out of gardens have also played a part in town planning. In this century the natural background has been given as much importance as buildings in developing the urban environment. In the last two decades the media of mass communication – advertising, traffic and other signs, television – have taken the place of idyllic nature and static architecture as environmental factors. Architecture has had to extend its frontiers: the new urban environment is Las Vegas, the town of neon lights, which Tom Wolfe, a critic of American culture, sees as the town of the twentieth century. It is a disappointment for those who, in the 1930's, believed that the methodical urban environment favoured by the functionalist architects would last for a thousand years.

The radicals of the 1930's were those who admired and adopted the cult of the machine; they believed that on the one hand it had created a new, irresistible style of architecture, different from anything that had gone before, and that on the other hand it was the fulfilment of all earlier technical and sociological development. It was architecture whose style was created out of the materials employed, steel or concrete.

It is largely on the laurels won by the bold spirits of the 1930's that the reputation of Finnish architecture still rests.

The history of modern architecture in Finland from the turn of the century until the present day is characterized by the same polarity between the evolution of the rationalists and the nostalgia of the romanticists as is found in European architecture in general. In addition to rationalism and romanticism the most significant ideological phenomena are internationalism and nationalism. These emotional attitudes have in turn determined the social purpose of the architect's work, a social purpose of which the measure is participation or alienation. In my view architects have seen their task as the need to satisfy the requirements of society, rather than to *change* society by their planning and design. Finnish architecture often seems to be an art form rather than a way of building; on the other hand the kinds of building that are spreading over the country at a far faster rate than the works of leading architects are not regarded as architecture. This contradiction stems from the fact that these aims are not sufficiently clearly defined.

One source of alienation is the romanticism that exists among architects themselves. Not all architecture that is created with feeling and that embodies subjective features is romantic. I would define as romantic the kind of architecture in which embellishment and ornamentation, either in the use of detail or in the whole, clearly contradict the rational function of the building. Rationalism must be interpreted widely. In addition to an awareness of social responsibility and economy of materials, we must also take into account an economy of artistic content, which, however, does not necessarily mean a scarcity of forms. The situation in architecture is quite different from that in the visual arts because observational-psychological factors require basic simplicity in a building or a plan. The idea must be visible. But it is possible to take simplification too far and in doing so to deprive the architectural environment of all variety and interest. This kind of exaggerated simplicity is very common in Finnish architecture of the fifties and sixties.

Romanticism is often linked with chauvinism, and this I would regard as the second kind of alienation. In a small country like Finland internationalism and nationalism have naturally played an important part; they have been the subject of much controversy and in the controversy they have come to represent very complex questions about the spiritual content of architecture. Nationalism was linked to the romanticism and the growing longing for independence that characterized the national romantic period at the beginning of this century; the shortsighted admiration of internationalism became apparent as functionalism began to break through.

At the height of the national romantic period Sigurd Frosterus' entry in the competition for the Helsinki railway station (1904) was criticised as architecture 'brought from abroad', in other words international rationalism. Students of the Technical University of Helsinki have been criticised in the sixties for adopting the style of Mies van der Rohe; the universal steel architecture of Mies is condemned because it is not part of the Finnish tradition.

Has the life force of Finnish architecture been rooted in national isolation?

6 The new architecture reached Finland in 1927. It is, however,

impossible to appreciate fully the situation in that year without first considering certain architectural developments that had occurred since the beginning of the century. It is a paradox that the international reputation of Finnish architecture was established partly as a result of nationally motivated romantic styles.

National Romanticism

The myth that there is a specifically Finnish style of architecture dates from the time it became necessary to employ every cultural device in defence of Finland's national identity. Eliel Saarinen's Finnish national architecture, which must have appeared on the Continent as primitivism full of fundamental energy, started to reach the attention of the public just at the time that *Art Nouveau* or *Jugendstil* was becoming a decadent form. Saarinen, like the composer Jean Sibelius and the painter Akseli Gallen-Kallela, drew his inspiration from the Finnish folk-epic, the *Kalevala,* whose nature-mysticism finds symbolic expression in his work. A positive feature in Saarinen's primitivism was its link with a national tradition; as a result his work was far more familiar than the European art that had been inspired by African or South Seas influences.

In one sense Finnish national romanticism was not an unexpected digression in the chain of development. Throughout Europe escapist romanticism frequently existed side by side with a striving after rationalism. For the great majority of people, who had experienced *Art Nouveau* as a superficial play of lines, the new style did not really mark an ethical revolution. Hence, although the national romantic movement arose in response to the need for national identity, much of the work it produced was acceptable to people all over Europe. Saarinen's interiors in water colour sketches, together with the work of the Scottish architect, C. R. Mackintosh, were popular exotic subjects in the pages of journals of interior decoration.

National romanticism started as a reform movement corresponding to and inspired by the English Arts and Crafts School in the 1890's. The development of open-plan design structures and materials took place in the shadow of medievalism and the search for a new aesthetic approach, and was not a simple, abstract rationalization.

Another important influence on this new movement was the American H. H. Richardson; his granite architecture had much in common with the Finnish medieval tradition. A synthesis of this kind – Arts and Crafts, Richardson and national consciousness – demanded an especially powerful force and ability to fuse them into a new whole. In this respect Saarinen and Lars Sonck, the other outstanding figure of the national romantic movement, represented only one aspect of Finnish architectural tradition.

Ever since the Middle Ages all architectural styles reaching Finland had been simplified while being adapted to local conditions. This gave birth to much refreshing primitivism: the simple basic form of the medieval churches and their rough walls, constructed of irregularly shaped boulders, were far removed from the Gothic tradition but nevertheless formed a plastic whole, an effect heightened by the naive but monumental interior wall paintings; the styles of the Renaissance and Baroque periods which were translated into wood in the hands of skilful local builders gave birth to an entirely new architecture. Even neoclassicism (also known as Empire Style) had a simplified 'Finnish' aspect in the works of Carl Ludvig Engel (1778-1840), who, though born and trained in Berlin, gained his most important experience of architecture in St. Petersburg.

This particularly Finnish response to influences from abroad occurs regularly in architecture from various other periods and can only be explained in terms of Finnish national temperament and climate. Hence it was only natural that at the turn of the century the younger generation should produce its own version of the continental *Art Nouveau*. Characteristic Finnish features of national romanticism were flora and fauna ornamentation and the use of granite or logs, which were not easily adaptable to new urban buildings. Nevertheless the winning designs for the Helsinki railway station were all reminiscent of medieval stone churches, as were the commercial buildings of Saarinen and Sonck, Romanticism favoured a rock-faced façade, which concealed a basic structure of brick and steel or concrete. The romantic movement did not introduce any structural advances, nor did it mark any advances in the architect's sense of social responsibility. It was architecture for the upper classes and made no attempt to find a solution to the housing problem that had arisen in the 1890's. National romanticism was not based on any indigenous architectural theory, but adopted certain of the rationalistic demands of the new movements in England and Belgium, such as the need for the façade to reflect the structural plan and the need to use genuine materials. Individual craftsmanship became the fashion for interiors – Henry van de Velde's views about mass production won no support at that time in Finland.

Although the Finnish national romantic movement did not influence events on the Continent, it did act as an important intellectual force in the other Scandinavian countries. We know from the Dane, Kay Fisker, that Finnish *avant garde* architecture, i.e. national romanticism, was considered to be so revolutionary that attempts were made to prevent Danish students of architecture from reading the Finnish architectural publication.

While continental *Art Nouveau* was fertilising Finnish national romanticism, Sonck was introducing to Finland the romantic town plans of the Austrian Camillo Sitte. Sonck's medievalism, however, did not bring any real improvement to the neo-Classic plan developed in the nineteenth century, in which towns were built up of square blocks of buildings laid out with gardens. It was true that the square block plan was unsuitable for hilly terrain, yet on the other hand a free form town plan with winding streets seemed unnatural on level ground.

International Rationalism

At the turn of the century the position in Finland was different from the rest of Europe. Industrialisation was still in its infancy and had not given rise to the sort of slums and housing problems that there were, for example, in Great Britain. The exciting challenge that large-scale industry meant for van de Velde was lacking. Although, if looked at from a modern viewpoint, Sigurd Frosterus' entry for the Helsinki railway station competition does not seem to have been brought in from abroad, it has an entirely different significance when considered in its historical context; the new aesthetic environment presented by Frosterus and Gustaf Strengell was a result of their declared programme of rationalisation and was intended to be the hub of a European metropolis similar to London or Berlin. In a Finnish context it was far ahead of its time, for Helsinki did not at that time even rank as a big city.

Sigurd Frosterus was one of those 'rare talents who were able to synthesize phenomena of their time'; he was a versatile observer of the cultural developments of his age and drew from both art and technology the elements that made up his all-embracing synthesis. Frosterus saw the turn of the century as the first period of modernism. In the light of new aesthetic values a sense of honesty was introduced to architecture, and the use of new materials in the forms to which they were most amenable slowly won approval – as Frosterus himself argued: 'The modern architect must slowly learn to see beauty in those forms to which he is driven by his sense of honesty.'

Sigurd Frosterus and Gustaf Strengell were the most conspicuous advocates in Finland of international rationalism. They had been 'saved' from romanticism by van de Velde's pronouncement on the ethical approach to the problem of planning. Most important of all they had to some extent personally experienced the evolution of the rationalists' 9 new aesthetics. In 1904 Strengell had seen a newspaper building in Amsterdam which had no ornamentation whatsoever on its glass façade; '... although 'aesthetically' ugly, the building was in its truthfulness ethically beautiful.'

In a small country like Finland resistance to romanticism was quick to take root. The romanticists and rationalists were no strangers to each other and it was impossible for the former not to respond to the logic of the rationalism. Saarinen, who had won the competition for the design of Helsinki railway station with an entry reminiscent of the National Museum, naturally appreciated the point of Frosterus' ideas. However, a construction reduced to the most basic essentials was a theoretical concept which at that time could not easily be put into practice. Moreover Frosterus, who advocated the use of steel frames, probably thought them to be limited in application, particularly as he himself had never used them. The use of concrete structures was still so new that neither Frosterus nor Saarinen could, in 1904, have seen in them the means of developing a new, constructive, 'honest' architecture.

Whereas in many respects national romantic architecture contained rationalist features, rationalist architects also employed romantic forms which contradicted aspects of their architectural programme. Frosterus' entry in the railway station competition contains, in the architectural context of 1904, much that is foreign; in both the overall effect and in detail there is clear evidence of the influence of van de Velde's ornamental forms. Indeed Frosterus drew up his design while working with van de Velde in Weimar and at the same time was working, among other things, on the plans for the Louis Dumont theatre. In the protest that Frosterus and Strengell published after the Station Competition (1904) one can discern among what is generally healthy rationalism, traces of groundless, consciously biased and controversial admiration of steel frames. Frosterus' writings reveal that he had only very limited practical experience of reinforced concrete frame construction, despite the fact that Selim A. Lindqvist had already been using frames of this kind in a completely modern form for some four years. It is not my intention to denigrate Frosterus' role as the most important exponent of the rationalist programme. Since, however, the starting point of this movement – the English Arts and Crafts movement and accompanying phenomena on the Continent – was not the private enclave of any one person but open to all, Saarinen, for example was just as ready as Frosterus at the time of the station competition to start building in the rationalist style. Saarinen was quicker to adopt the use of reinforced concrete frames, without becoming involved in theorizing.

10   Saarinen, who was more of an intellectual and more alert than Sonck,

changed his style as early as 1904. Evidence of this can be seen in the Molchow-Haus built in Germany (1905-7) which is an excellent example of the Viennese post-*Jugendstil*. Helsinki railway station, for which the plans were completed in 1909, reveals even more clearly the influence of objective architecture. By this date Saarinen was more familiar with reinforced concrete construction and the completed station is more constructivist than the design submitted to the competition by Frosterus.

Sonck, who in Tampere Cathedral (1902-6) and the Helsinki telephone building (1905) created the most outstanding monuments of the national romantic movement, gradually came to follow Saarinen's lead and started to construct his façades of stones hewn far smoother than before. The Mortgage Bank building (1908) has separate round columns which are ornamented with romantic capitals. The Stock Exchange building (1911) has a structurally differentiated smooth granite façade.

It is generally thought that both romanticism and rationalism were forced to yield to regressive classicism. This view appears to be based mainly on Sonck's later development. It could equally well be argued that rationalism, which, starting in 1904 became increasingly dominant even in the work of former romanticists, finally led to wholly constructivist solutions in which the structure was reduced to a minimum, the use of glass surfaces increased and the structural form became the only aesthetic factor – structure became synonymous with beauty. If Sonck is not regarded as the standard by whom all others are assessed it can be shown that progressive rationalism did not yield, but remained the dominating style. Sonck returned to the classical colonnade; the time had not yet come when a simple reinforced concrete column could be used – or, to be more precise, the fashionable architects of the period were not ready to use this device.

The Pioneer of Concrete Architecture

The serious development of structural forms had no part in the conflicts between exponents of romantic and rationalist architecture. Indeed the process of development was so undramatic that only in retrospect have we become aware of the course it followed.

Steel frames were already in use in the nineteenth century, although they were usually hidden from sight beneath the building's outer skin. The earliest cast iron construction in Finland is probably found in the columns and girders of the Finlayson factory and date from 1837. From the late 1880's leading architects used steel frames in their larger works 11 as a means of roofing over large spaces or as the framework for glass roofs; such frames were usually imported from abroad. Well-known examples of this approach are the National Gallery of Art *(Ateneum)* designed by Carl Theodor Höijer and Gustaf Nyström's House of Estates *(Säätytalo)* and the headquarters of the former *Yhdyspankki*. The internal frame of the State Archives *(Valtionarkisto)* is wholly of steel, and to retain a structural consistency Nyström also designed a constructivist column façade reminiscent of the industrial buildings of early functionalism.

Gustaf Nyström taught for many years at the Technical University in Helsinki and at the turn of the century was training the younger generation, including Saarinen and Frosterus. Although Nyström's buildings are almost without exception neo-Renaissance in style, his experience in the use of steel and, later, reinforced concrete frames, inevitably influenced his students.

Hence the development of new structures has its origin in neo-Renaissance architecture both as an experiment in steel construction and as a constructivist expression of the façade. At the beginning of the twentieth century Selim A. Lindqvist, the most important innovator of new structures, provided through his concrete architecture closer links than any other of the national romanticists between the neo-Renaissance movement and functionalism.

Lindqvist was the child prodigy of architecture. When only twenty-two years old he designed the façades of a commercial and residential building whose plans had been drafted by the progressive Elia Heikel. In this building, and later in the Lundqvist commercial building, Lindqvist developed from the various structures already at the architect's disposal a completely modern construction with a pillar framework and large display windows.

Frosterus contrasted Lindqvist's modern commercial buildings with the anachronistic granite palaces of Saarinen and Sonck; Frosterus had his office in the Lundqvist building, which also provided a meeting place for the internationally minded Euterpe club. Lindqvist was not satisfied with the aesthetic expression of the structures in common use and began to investigate the possibilities of reinforced concrete. It has not been explained whether Lindqvist became the pioneer of the use of reinforced concrete in Finnish architecture merely as a result of his 'artistic' instinct, nor is it clear whether the constructivism of neo-Renaissance buildings led him to discover the characteristics of the new material, since Lindqvist published no programme of work nor did he explain the motives behind his designs. In 1900 he made the first horizontal concrete slab and began to use concrete as a visible part of a structure. The

Suvilahti power station (1908)(I) is an early reinforced concrete building comparable to the works of the Frenchman, Auguste Perret.

The modernity of Lindqvist's work was neither controversial nor violent and in this respect was unlike that of the Austrian, Adolf Loos. The Viennese architects provide a good point of comparison because at the end of the first decade of this century Lindqvist's architecture became increasingly sensitive, used finer lines and became more structuralist. The *Villa Ensi* (1911), reminiscent of Josef Hoffmann's work, marks the culmination of these individual attempts at abstraction.

The development of rationalism in Finland was largely stimulated by the corresponding movement on the continent. The ideas of the Finns did not influence the architects of any other countries; this is particularly true of Selim Lindqvist, the architect whose work might have been of real significance. Likewise the ideas emanating from the German *Werkbund* received relatively little attention in Finland after Frosterus, at the beginning of this century, had come into contact with the arts and crafts school van de Velde had founded in Weimar. The essential question is whether the rationalists were even more isolated than the romanticists from what was happening in Europe.

In the dialectic stage of development at the beginning of the century Frosterus, as a theoretician, is to some extent the counterpart of Loos; he realised that new materials such as galvanized metal sheets were just as acceptable from the point of view of architectural aesthetics as a tiled roof. But no single Finn possessed all the qualities that characterised Loos: in Frosterus one found the theoretician, in Lindqvist the constructivist and in Onni Tarjanne the rationalist. No Finn ever set himself so openly against prevailing aesthetic opinion as the anarchistic Loos.

Art Nouveau to Functionalism

Changes in style often divert attention from more fundamental developments, and in this respect they can be misleading. Of the various conflicting 'isms' during the first decade of this century there survived many positive features that were to have a lasting effect. In the second decade still greater stylistic innovations were introduced. Finnish architects, like their counterparts in Sweden, turned to the historical 'practical architecture' of Italy in their search for some kind of guide towards the establishment of an aesthetic standard; in the development of rationalism an approach sensitive to social problems gained the upper hand at the expense of structural refinement. Characteristic of these new atti-   13 tudes were the use of heavy, bare walls with small windows, and limited ornamentation carefully placed to heighten the overall effect.

The campaign of the Swede, Gregor Paulsson for 'more beautiful utensils' illustrates the sense of social responsibility that began to permeate both the design of ordinary utensils and architecture. In this respect rationalism, which at the beginning of the century was by its very nature far less conspicuous than either national romanticism or *Jugendstil* constructivism, proved to be the most lasting stylistic tradition. Onni Tarjanne's design for the Takaharju sanatorium (1903) is just as much 'denuded' architecture as the rational classicism of the 1910's and 1920's. The term 'romantic classicism', despite its apparent contradiction in terms, probably illustrates most aptly the prevailing character of the period.

The decades before functionalism are generally regarded as insignificant in terms of historical development. Nevertheless it was during this period that architects were becoming conscious of the new state of society and were beginning to see their architecture in terms of the functioning of that society. This period anticipated functionalism socially rather than structurally. The practical aspects of architecture were consciously emphasized; aesthetic features were not abandoned, their ever-changing aesthetic norm was merely created anew.

The 1910's and the 1920's were in fact of greater importance than the 1930's, when functionalism actually put into practice what the preceding decades had prepared. The new approach did not suddenly appear in 1927 as the result of foreign influence, but was simply the continuation of a process of development reaching back to the *Jugendstil* rationalism at the beginning of this century. There existed the need for a new architecture even before the basic forms of functionalism spread to Finland from France, Germany and Holland. During the 1920's certain new features had already evolved independently in Finland, features such as the abandonment of ornamentation, a free floor plan, an articulated structure, all of which were canonized by the functionalists. It was the leading architects who were the quickest to adopt functionalism and in their work they developed a new kind of simplicity and a new sense of social responsibility. The relationship of the 1920's with functionalism was almost the same as that of the 1890's with the *Jugendstil* movement; in both cases a healthy rationalist process was already under way, a tendency which was subsequently embodied by the new stylistic breakthrough. The main difference is that the architects who adopted functionalism in the 1920's – Aalto, Bryggman, Ekelund, Pauli E. Blomstedt – became the leading exponents of the new style.

14 From the point of view of rationalism it was not a question of a revolution

in style but simply a confirmation and consolidation of the direction in which it was already moving.

Hilding Ekelund drew the attention of architects to another aspect in which architecture of the 1920's bore some similarity to that of the turn of the century: there are obvious romantic traits in the architecture of the 1920's, both periods displayed a preference for genuine surface materials. It was only in its more traditional handling of detail, a regular axial symmetry and a straightness of line that the architecture of the 1920's differed from that of the turn of the century. The asymmetry that evolved in the 1920's anticipated functionalism in that it led to a less strictly defined open-plan design. This reflects the conflicts in which one becomes involved if functionalism is understood literally as simply rationalist architecture whose form and content are determined by the practical purpose of a building. If, on the other hand, we think of functionalism as being a similar kind of style as, for example, *Jugendstil*, then it becomes possible to appreciate how Le Corbusier — and gradually Mies van der Rohe — regarded functionalism as a new classicism, which the former even compared to ancient Greek architecture. The characteristics of functionalism in Finland were almost the same as those of *Jugendstil*: asymmetry and the dividing of a building plastically into effective masses.

The fact that the nostalgic classicism of the 1920's appears to display a more conscious sense of social responsibility than functionalism gives rise to a second contradiction. The interest of designers in housing problems and the environment in which people must live goes back to the 1910's. The town plan for the Töölö area of Helsinki also specified to what extent the yard area enclosed by the buildings should be developed; this led to coherent blocks built around large, open courtyards. The block of flats designed by Armas Lindgren for the workers of a factory in Vallila (another part of Helsinki) is the finest example of this humanitarian approach.

The English garden suburb idea was an important influence. One of the most significant results of this inspiration, the Käpylä garden suburb (1920-5) [2] in Helsinki, is in many ways an outstanding monument to the architecture of the beginning of the century. The overall plan, drawn up by Birger Brunila and Otto-Iivari Meurman, recalls in various ways the formal composition of the English garden suburb, especially the small open spaces formed by grouping the houses together. Martti Välikangas attempted to introduce the maximum amount of standardisation to the houses he designed. The basic plan of the houses does away completely with classical axial symmetry — as a student Välikangas had been in the forefront of those who favoured asymmetrical compo- 15 sitions – and results in dwellings that are particularly comfortable to live in. Today the residential environment of Käpylä is one of the most pleasant and most unspoiled in Finland.

The change from this organic rationalism to an ideologically conscious functionalism is an interesting phase, interesting because of the way in which people became aware of functionalism. From the point of view of style the difference between the classicism and functionalism of the 1920's is obvious, but despite this a large number of architects were still able to accept functionalism as a phenomenon which was a direct consequence of what had gone before, just as if no revolution had taken place.

This stylistic change crept in unnoticed about the middle of the 1920's. Aalto and Bryggman, in their interiors, used the electric light fittings of the Dane, Poul Henningsen and the same kind of Viennese chairs as Le Corbusier. These influences were not seen as the signs of a new and separate style, but were absorbed into the classicism of the 1920's. Sigurd Frosterus had obtained copies of Le Corbusier's earliest books the moment they appeared in the 1920's. In his work *Rakennus taide-luomana* (The Building as an Artistic Creation, 1928) Strengell devoted a whole chapter to Le Corbusier. Although he listed the French architect's theories about aesthetic factors, structural refinement, engineer architecture and standardization, he did not publish a single specimen of Le Corbusier's work, which meant that these new ideas did not make so effective an impact as might have been possible.

Hence although Le Corbusier's name was known during the second half of the 1920's, the new architecture did not reveal itself in all its glory. An important link between the Continent and Finland was the Danish *Kritisk Revy* (Critical Review) published by Poul Henningsen. The journal was not only opposed to the conservative *Arkitekten* (The Architect), the official Danish architectural publication, but frequently attacked with equal zeal academicism in general, capitalism, and the Church. Finland had nothing that could be compared to this; the nearest thing to Poul Henningsen was Alvar Aalto, who, among radical architects, was one of the most left-wing. He also wrote for the *Kritisk Revy*, although his subject, the construction of cinema walls, was politically neutral. At no stage before the Second World War did architectural 'leftism' ever appear to be connected with political leftism.

Since every leading Finnish architect in the 1920's was involved in the process of development from classicism to functionalism, there was none who could achieve Henningsen's detachment from events and see this progressive liberalism in perspective. In Finland, however, academicism was not so rigid as in Denmark nor were architects so tightly grouped according to age. Moreover, the Finnish journal *Arkkitehti* (The Architect) was in the hands of the progressives. In 1927 Carolus Lindberg, who taught History of Architecture at the Technical University of Helsinki, was gently eased out as editor, and his place was taken by Martti Välikangas; although the new editor had not introduced functionalist features into his own work, he had been amongst the most progressive thinkers ever since his student days. He had also been responsible for the planning of Käpylä. One of Välikangas' editorial assistants was Hilding Ekelund.

The Swedish journal *Byggmästaren* (The Masterbuilder) was giving wide coverage to Le Corbusier as early as 1926 and Uno Åhren, while still in the middle of the classical period, borrowed the Frenchman's words: 'And now as we invade new and hitherto unforeseen spheres with the calculations and machines which help and force us forward so our hearts yearn for the past'. The pictures that were published of Le Corbusier's buildings, however, for example the Vaucresson villa, could just as easily have conveyed a picture of well balanced rationalism as of unrestrained modernism.

The Finnish journal *Arkkitehti* did not print any pictures of functionalist buildings before the publication, in 1929, of those of Aalto's Standard block of flats in Turku. It can hardly be said that functionalism reached Finland as the result of an extensive publicity campaign.

The need to find some kind of rational solution became increasingly urgent towards the end of the 1920's. Although constructivism was pushing neo-classicism aside, the problems of style still appeared to be overwhelming. Aalto's Workers' Club House (1925) [3] in Jyväskylä, is eloquent evidence of this search for a more honest architecture. The upper part of the building is blank, in the prevailing style, exceptionally so, whereas the lower part, based on the classical colonnade theme, is open, with large glass surfaces. Pauli E. Blomstedt's bank building in Helsinki, completed in 1930, has a solution similar to that of Frosterus' design for the Stockmann department store [4]: columns extend over the whole façade making the building violently vertical.

1930 also saw the completion of Oiva Kallio's Northern Union building *(Pohjayhtiön talo)* in Helsinki [5]. The change from total verticalism to total horizontalism would appear, in view of its significance, to be an enormous step. Nevertheless Kallio's building was modern in a perfectly natural way – despite certain traces of the classicism of the 1920's.

Hence Blomstedt's bank building was completed at a critical moment in the process of change. The upper part of the banking hall is surrounded by a blank wall surface for which some kind of mural decoration was 17 planned. The effect perfectly epitomized the ideals of the 1920's. But on returning from abroad Blomstedt removed with one stroke the mural decoration from his drawings so that nowadays the wall area has a functionalist, horizontal appearance.

Revolution in Architecture

The new architecture, known by the simple name of functionalism, reached Finland in 1927, the year that saw its European breakthrough in the Weissenhofsiedlung housing exhibition at Stuttgart. It was immediately recognized by most architects as a new architectural style, although it was in reality merely the fulfilment of the striving towards rationalism of preceding decades. The pioneers at the beginning of the century had been moving towards only one facet of functionalism and not the kind of functionalism characteristic of Walter Gropius and Le Corbusier.

Functionalism is a concept that can be interpreted in many ways. The Americans Horatio Greenough and Louis Sullivan had felt the need for some kind of 'functionalism' in the architecture of the previous century and Sullivan had developed his own rationalist approach. Initially the European functionalism of the 1920's followed the example of Gropius and Le Corbusier whose reinforced concrete constructions made possible the new socially conscious attitude. Technical progress and this new attitude joined together to point the way to the fulfillment of popular need by means of standardization and mass prefabrication.

On the Continent functionalism was a direct continuation of Henry van de Velde's early machine culture and as such aimed at the mass production of cheap, high quality goods by mechanical processes. In this respect modernism is to be regarded as one of the serious spasms of conscience in 150 years of industrialization.

In Finland functionalism was the answer to the rationalist programme of Frosterus and Strengell and to what Lindqvist was already intuitively seeking; at the same time it was organically a part of the rationalist aspirations inherent in the classicism of the 1920's. These factors would of themselves have resulted in functionalism had there been in Finland a radical comparable to Gropius. In Finland it was not the young, newly qualified architects who established functionalism; although the pioneers of the new style were relatively young (Aalto was about 30 at the time of his monumental works, the Viipuri Library and the Paimio Sanatorium), they had all been active in the 1920's and had gained a reputation before they turned to functionalism.

In these circumstances it is not surprising that functionalism quickly found supporters among Finnish architects. In 1928 Blomstedt, who was later to become the most 'Corbusian' of Finnish architects, was scornful about how easily the change from classicism took place:

'Yesterday we regarded functionalism as merely "an expression of the well known tastelessness of the French, Germans and Dutch" – tomorrow it will be "culture" – because today it has been approved in Stockholm. In any case the change to the "Corbusier style" will hardly be difficult for us. We already know about thin shapes, asymmetry is well on the way to becoming orthodox doctrine – away with meanders and palmettes and more horizontal lines in the façade.'

Functionalism had been stimulated by industrial buildings, in which, especially in the United States, rationalism had evolved spontaneously at a very early date. Gropius' Fagus factory (1911) in Alfeld, Germany, is generally regarded as the earliest example; in the 1930's too, industrial buildings continued to play an important role in the development of functionalism, for industry has always been among the first to adopt simpler and more practical structures. In Sweden the architectural office, the Cooperative Union Corporation, was foremost in employing the new style and was almost as bold in its projects as the Soviet constructivist architects. Likewise in Finland Erkki Huttunen, who designed industrial buildings for the State Alcohol Monopoly and SOK (a chain of stores with its own production, packaging and distribution complex) [14], was allowed to employ unadulterated functionalism.

The Aesthetics of Functionalism

By the beginning of this century industrialization had created so many new forms and shapes – shapes resulting from technical advances, new styles of dress, etc. – that the main features of the 'style of the age' had been obscured. Although exponents of *Art Nouveau* regarded it as a new, unifying style in the same way as the neo-Renaissance, the most far-sighted of contemporary observers, such as Frosterus in Finland, saw the need to develop a new kind of aesthetics – sufficiently comprehensive to embrace all possible phenomena, to admit the possibility of beauty in everything (including machines, transport, sport etc).

Functionalism was the style that was wholly founded on industrial forms and production processes, which consciously took a modernistic attitude towards life. The German *Bauhaus* provided the widest range of technical aesthetics that extended to every form of art. The functionalists realized that they had at last a style applicable to those processes that had been evolving during the previous 150 years and that this new style had come to stay.   19

But in their eagerness to show that beauty is also possible in completely rationalist architecture, or in the design of utensils, the functionalists stretched their aesthetics to the extreme, with the result that functionalism moved so far from its original standpoint that it became as distant from ordinary people as *Art Nouveau* had been in its time. Ekelund regarded the dramatisation of masses and detail as characteristic of the architecture of the 1920's. This trait was inherited by functionalism which, particularly in Finland, became the heroic period of white architecture. Emphasis was placed on horizontalism, especially in industrial buildings and warehouses, whose narrow strips of windows became the hallmark of functionalist utilitarian architecture. The kind of boldness that reaches such heights in the Stadium Tower [19] and the main elevation of the Paimio Sanatorium [7] has not been achieved in later architecture.

Functionalism was a great attempt to create a uniform, definitive architecture, applicable anywhere in the world, to create something that was different from all previous aesthetic styles. Although functionalism was firmly rooted in social theory, the number of qualitatively good buildings it produced throughout Europe is distressingly small; instead of being the products of anonymous mass production, as required by functionalist theory, they have become individual works of art known to all. Particularly rare are large areas devoted exclusively to functionalist architecture. The only examples in Finland are the Sunila factory [13] and its residential complex and the Helsinki Olympic Village [18]. All other examples of functionalist architecture exist as isolated 'monuments'.

Or does this only apply to the works of better known architects? Did there evolve during the 1920's and thirties a widespread socially conscious architecture of which the products merge anonymously into the background? In Helsinki, for example, Central Töölö was built in the 1930's; the houses are uniform, unpretentious grey functionalism. The façades of the houses reveal at once the main features of the basic plan: the living room extends farther outwards than the other rooms and has a large window. Although the houses lack any architectural characteristic, their standard of detail is higher and more beautiful than that of today in glass, wood and nickel-plated steel.

Functionalism in Finland did not produce any clear-cut theory. Some general axioms were published, but these were remarkably similar to the requirements of rationalism at the beginning of the century, e.g. that the façade should reflect the internal division of a building. Apart from this a number of practical requirements were put forward concerning materials and the solution of living space. Social conscience was

20

much in evidence, and as a result of German influence it frequently expressed itself in peculiar forms – e.g. in recommending the minimum dwelling as a generally ideal solution irrespective of the measures that had to be taken because of the housing problem. The social approach of functionalism was often mechanical; idealism was architectural idealism and not a sense of social responsibility. There were, however, exceptions: in the housing estates Aalto designed for industrial communities a humanitarian aim can clearly be discerned: the worker was entitled to a home every bit as well designed as that of the well-to-do townsman.

In 1931 Ekelund wrote in his review of a book by the Swede Gustaf Näsström:

'Contemporary Swedish "functionalism" is an overwhelming phenomenon both from a quantitative and a qualitative point of view. Quantitative because nearly all the most outstanding younger architects support it . . . Qualitative because it has effectively adopted the healthy theoretical content of the new schools of thought yet without following the example of the romantic modernists and seeking "modern" effects at any price, nor attempting to emulate the rather metaphysical or formalist rationalism of some Germans . . .'

For the Swedes the German influence was considerably more important than that of the French and led to their adopting social objectives, 'the new reality' *(die neue Sachlichkeit),* and to using technical advances as instruments of the welfare state. The poetry of Le Corbusier was too lyrical for the spirit of social revolution associated with the breakthrough of functionalism in Sweden. The Swedish journal *Spektrum* published many articles and debates about social questions including Gunnar Myrdal's essay on the expropriation of land.

Many aspects of this attitude spread to Finland and found expression in the work and writings of Aalto, (Aalto published an article in *Spektrum* about the 'geography' of the housing problem in which the mythical approach towards methods of communication anticipated Marshall McLuhan). Nevertheless, Finnish functionalism was – if one excludes Gunnar Asplund's Stockholm exhibition (1930) – decisively more conscious of aesthetic values, and, at the same time, more expressive and more elegant than Swedish architecture of the 1930's. This pattern of development in Finland was also to be significant in determining the direction of Finnish architecture in the years after the Second World War, a period in which Swedish architecture lagged almost twenty years behind that of Finland.

Reference has frequently been made to the contribution of the 21 rationalists at the beginning of this century to the eventual form functionalism was to take. In addition to Frosterus' views already mentioned, Strengell published very early on (1901) an aesthetic theory with ethical overtones: ' . . . a demand for complete honesty, structural simplicity and practical suitability. These factors are at the same time an expression of the new ideals of beauty.' The stylistic transition of 1930 is to be compared with the transition from neo-Renaissance to *Jugendstil* rationalism at the turn of the century. Concurrent with both these changes structural and social development were continuing so that the new style appeared to influence only superficial stylistic features. The most important aspect of these transitional periods, however, was the way in which they changed attitudes: people came to realize that a new age had begun, technical and social factors showed themselves to be parts of the same order of things. These changes also brought with them a new ethical responsibility; architecture ceased to be merely a question of aesthetics. In such circumstances it was natural that the housing question should come to the fore, especially towards the end of the 1920's when the problem had become most acute, as, among other causes, the effect of industrial expansion on the growth of towns began to make itself seriously felt.

In 1932 Ekelund produced the following synthesis of the various factors that characterised the new architecture:

'The aesthetic approach to architecture was replaced by a new approach which put greater emphasis on reality; the need to design homes for workers, factories and blocks of flats brought home to the architect the seriousness of his profession, his responsibility to society and his obligations . . . classicism has had to give way more and more to practical solutions to architectural problems and nowadays it can be said that "functionalism" . . . has become the main factor in the thinking of Finnish architects.'

The New Architecture

The characteristic features of functionalism were first seen in public in the competition plans submitted by Erik Bryggman in 1927 for a commercial building in Vaasa. In the window strip of the perspective plan, in the lines of the cars speeding by, the image of the new era is evident for the first time; it is modern in the same way as a Continental railway station, with its trains and sensibly dressed, hurrying people, had been modern to Frosterus and Strengell at the turn of the century. The de-
22 cisive factor was not that the Vaasa building would have represented,

had it ever been built, a compromise between the style of the 1920's and functionalism, but that the overall effect revealed that a change in attitude had taken place.

In the same year Alvar Aalto won the first prize in the competition for the Viipuri Library. His design clearly reflects the influence of the Swede, Gunnar Asplund in the 1920's, on Finnish architecture. Asplund's design for the Stockholm municipal library had won the admiration of Finnish architects; its elementarist classicism had points of contact with the pre-functionalist atmosphere. Asplund's Stockholm exhibition buildings (1930) were the most conspicuous manifesto of functionalism in Scandinavia. In Aalto's design the Viipuri Library was conceived as a simple building whose symmetry was broken by the main entrance. The interior division of space was unrestrainedly axial, though at the same time the asymmetric layout of the rooms satisfied administrative requirements. The Helsinki Art Hall (1926), *Taidehalli,* designed by Ekelund and Jarl Eklund, displayed, despite its basic classicism, a similar elastic asymmetry.

This pre-functionalism was architecturally not unlike Le Corbusier's early works; his view that 'architecture is the splendid play of forms in light' refers more to the concept of forms as classically pure and powerful, than to the social aspects of an architectural problem.

In 1928 Aalto's entry won the competition for the design of the Paimio Sanatorium. Aalto's plan was entirely modern and required no modification when the building was erected. In the interval between competing for the Viipuri Library and the Paimio Sanatorium Aalto came under the influence of the Stuttgart *Weissenhofsiedlung* and Gropius' *Bauhaus* which resulted in his total conversion to modernism. The sanatorium [7] gained an international reputation for Finnish architecture; as Sigfried Giedion has observed, the building generally consolidated the belief in the potential of functionalism. The open basic plan, with the various parts of the building branching off according to function, is reminiscent of Gropius' *Bauhaus* building, which was similarly a freely grouped composition.

This intermediate stage in Aalto's development also produced changes in the plans for the Viipuri library [8]. Nevertheless the building remains a remarkable compromise between classicism and functionalism – an especially fruitful compromise which occupies a key role in tracing the relationship between these styles. The uniform scheme was divided into two parallel masses; one housed the borrowing department and lending rooms, the other the entrance, lecture hall and offices. Ekelund has described how, as a student, Välikangas was interested in the problem of fitting together two parallel blocks of different heights. A similar

23

arrangement appears in the Workers' Building designed by the Russian Kasimir Malevitch (1925) in which the traffic axis runs in the opposite direction to that of the main masses, in the same way as in Aalto's library. At a later date Aulis Blomstedt used a similar 'contrapuntal' solution in his Workers' Institute in Helsinki and in a proposal for a library in Turku.

The overall solution of Aalto's library was impressive: the new ceiling lighting solution made it possible to provide the lending department and the reading rooms with windowless walls. This higher and wider part of the building is designed so that the interior layout can easily be deduced from outside: the lending department is on a slightly higher level than the reading rooms; stairs separate the newspaper room from the study room. So large a block without a single window was naturally a bold achievement, though in spirit closer to the classicism of the 1920's — and the original entry for the competition — than to the modern quest for open space.

The first expressions of functionalism are located in Turku, where Bryggman had his home and where Aalto went to live in the late 1920's. In a short time these two architects developed the new rationalism straight into its classical stage. They became conscious of the structural nature of reinforced concrete architecture and the characteristics of functionalism derived from it; their enthusiasm lasted until the end of the 1930's. Aalto and Bryggman both prepared excellent plans for various competitions, often entering for the same competition, and both had their share of success. Bryggman's entry for the head office of the Suomi insurance company in Helsinki (1927) was almost a variant of Aalto's building for the Turku newspaper *Turun Sanomat*. In 1929 they co-operated on the exhibition buildings to celebrate Turku's 700th anniversary, a far more modest manifesto of functionalism than the exhibition in Stockholm the following year. The Stockholm exhibition was a victory for the Finnish, as much as for the Swedish modernists, and Aalto wrote admiringly in *Arkkitehti* of Gunnar Asplund's achievement.

The new style gained an increasingly firm foothold. This acceptance was made all the easier by the fact that young architects were usually the judges in the competition and themselves shared the views of the competitors. Various bodies requiring new buildings displayed a commendable lack of prejudice in accepting modern ideas. Architects also received private commissions, of which the most important were Aalto's Standard block of flats in Turku (1927-9) and the premises of the *Turun Sanomat* (1930). The Standard block of flats achieved the modernization of its kind. Although in its more neutral functionalism the basic plan reveals certain characteristics of the 1920's, Aalto achieved in this work the modernization of this particular kind of dwelling two years before the Stockholm exhibition.

The building for the *Turun Sanomat* [6] was the first project in Finland to realize Le Corbusier's five-point plan: a building supported on columns, an internal reinforced concrete framework, horizontal strip windows, a free plan and a roof garden (in this particular case, more terrace than garden). The building is the purest example of early functionalism in Finland.

A local journalist wrote of the Standard block of flats:

'A functionalist building – the first of its kind in Finland; not even Sweden has come as far as we have, (for that country did not produce its first two functionalist buildings until some time later): the façade is in a completely new style with horizontal windows and modest simple surfaces'.

Functionalism began in Finland as international modernism. Aalto, who in the context of the 1920's had begun to express his own personality within the scope of classicism, assumed in Finland the role of the international modernist. He represented all those ideas that are associated with functionalism in its widest sense: internationalism, democratization, collectivism and industrial productivity theories. Aalto's reputation does not rest on the same factors as Eliel Saarinen's; his works were not primarily specimens of indigenous architecture, but belonged to the youthful tradition of continental functionalism.

The need to create something strictly Finnish arose later, partly as a result of the use of wood. I regard the Finnish pavilions at the exhibitions in Paris (1936) and New York (1939) [10] as just this kind of national monument.

Aalto's pioneer work in the 1930's represented a genuinely new approach to design. He rejected what had hitherto been generally accepted, both products and concepts, and thought out everything anew. Among the reasons for this was, of course, the need to find a personal form of expression, an attempt to achieve stylistic coherence; not even the Thonet chair was acceptable, for that had its own history. Aalto designed a range of furniture out of bent and glued wood, and he designed his own light fittings and vases.

Aalto's pioneer work was not in itself unique. Modernists had already provided new styles in furniture so that people could furnish their homes in keeping with their architectural style. Functionalism would have been a stylistic compromise, had it failed to consider furniture design. Production of functionalist furniture, however, acquired at once a wide ethical-social significance. By this time the in- 25 dustrial revolution had reached the point where mass production was a viable proposition, a situation of which men, including Henry van de Velde, had dreamed but had not been able to bring about. The age of cheap but tasteful furniture had begun; the character of the functionalist interior was 'ideal economy', and it was equally available to both rich and poor. The most important designers were Marcel Breuer who specialized in metal furniture, and Aalto, who started by designing in metal, but later, mainly in connection with his work on the Viipuri Library and the Paimio Sanatorium, created his world-renowned wooden furniture. Metal furniture did not win great favour in Finland, where it was regarded as too cold for the home (a view shared by Poul Henningsen in Denmark).

Nowadays, thirty years later, the most essential feature of this revolutionary spirit has been forgotten; a new social division has evolved and heavy, expensive furniture is now designed for the well-to-do. In Finland both Breuer's and Mies van der Rohe's steel furnishings are now a part of the fashionable interior, and priced accordingly. Aalto's furniture has best retained its original social character and his ordinary mass-produced chairs are as cheap and popular as ever.

Aalto was clearly inspired by the *Bauhaus,* which took a radical new look at the design of all types of materials. In contrast to the collective spirit of the *Bauhaus,* Finnish architects tended to work on their own and had no corresponding centre of activity from which new ideas could permeate to others in the same field. Within the framework of international functionalism Aalto created his own personal style. This style, of which the most obvious characteristic is its so-called 'free form', is often regarded as expressive and irrational; however, the curving shapes of his wooden furniture, for example, are the result of a technical solution. It results from a way of joining vertical and horizontal constructive members. At the most one can speak of the preference for form; one can say that Aalto chooses the particular technical solution that produces the required form. Hence in his 'free-form' architecture [11] the form simply occurs, as a result of the technical considerations; similarly the amoeba-like shape of his glass vases [12] are not necessarily a result of the production method. But the disciplined and exciting curved form of the Helsinki House of Culture (1958) [27], for example, does not appear in the least arbitrary.

During the 1930's Aalto was fortunate enough to receive a large number of commissions; he created an imposing range of buildings which are all significant in some new way. Aalto designed, in conjunction with his work on the Sunila cellulose factory [13], a complete housing estate – such developments were one of the most favoured manifestations of functionalism. In the Sunila project he was able to experiment with various types of dwellings: three-storied terraced blocks of flats, in which each flat has its own entrance, as well as a luxurious block that spreads out like a fan. The Sunila estate with its white houses set amongst the forest is one of the largest uniform units produced in Finland by the 'Heroic' architecture of the 1930's.

Several works had their origin as the winning entries in architectural competitions. Aalto's entries were always fresh in approach and had been subjected to a thorough examination. Many of his suggestions failed to win approval and were never built, among them his proposal for a museum of the arts in Tallinn (1936) [9] in which the layout and skilfully divided compact mass anticipated later, more complicated, buildings.

Functionalism and Traditionalism

In 1931 Aalto applied for the Chair of Architecture in Helsinki, but the post went to Johan Sigfrid Sirén who continued to work in a rigidly classical style long into the 1930's and never designed a genuinely modern building. Naturally there has been much speculation about the possible development of Finnish architecture had the training of young architects been Aalto's responsibility for the last three decades. Sirén's reputation rests largely on his design for the Parliament House; the functionalists poured scorn on this nationalist monument, although as such it displays a sound sense of form and brought together the best artists and interior designers in the country to create a stylistically harmonious whole. Hilding Ekelund – then editor of *Arkkitehti* – described the building in the following terms:

'The Parliament House is an anthem to the monumental; architecture in which the basic principle has been art for art's sake; aesthetically its creator had a completely free hand and the beauty of its form is an end in itself. Hence this building is consciously in contrast to the new, socially motivated attitudes permeating architecture . . .'

Many years later (1962) Ekelund confirmed his view that the building marked the end of the stylistic era of the 1920's and that rarely had a building in Finland been built with such architectural consistency, technical skill and stylistic enthusiasm.

In 1931 Sirén also won the competition for the enlargement of the University of Helsinki and built an extension to Engel's neo-Classical building which was, to a large extent, merely a less interesting copy of the original. Several functionalists also entered the same competition 27 and one of them, Pauli E. Blomstedt, suggested that a hallway should extend through the four floors of the new building, a solution that could, in the most refined way, have reproduced the theme of the entrance hall in Engel's main building.

The competition brought J.S. Sirén and the journal *Arkkitehti* into frequent conflict, often very personal in nature; the journal also began to direct its criticism against conservatism in other competitions, in particular competitions for the design of new churches. Conservatism and functionalism clashed in 1931 in the competition for the Lallukka Artists' Building, in which the first two prizes were awarded to conservative entries. Ekelund criticized the decisions and published a wide selection of the modern entries that had received no prize. As a result of public criticism Gösta Juslen's functionalist suggestion was in fact subsequently accepted and built.

The main clash occurred at the end of 1932 as a result of the competition for a church to be built in the Tehtaanpuisto park, in south Helsinki. The rules of the competition required that attention be paid 'to the wish of the Church Commissioners that architecturally the building be in keeping with traditional church forms'. As Ekelund pointed out in *Arkkitehti,* this condition bore fruit. Sonck, Liljekvist and Sirén, who all submitted conventionally classical designs, were judged winners of the competition. The same edition of the journal contained a discussion by Strengell on traditionalism and functionalism in worship and church buildings. Strengell points to the amusing dichotomy of the Lutheran service with, on the one hand the resplendent communion service at the altar reminiscent of the Catholic Church, and on the other the sermon preached by someone clad in formal black attire. He wonders whether 'in such circumstances it could ever be possible to give Lutheran Church architecture a rational, modern form in keeping with its functions'.

The Architect and Society

Apart from those particular competitions, in which for reasons of tradition the modernists did not win recognition, the leading functionalists received a relatively free hand to put their ideas into practice. An important factor in making this possible was doubtless the very respected social position that architects had enjoyed in Finland ever since the beginning of the century. It had been suggested within C. I. A. M. (Les Congrés Internationaux d'Architecture Moderne) that the architect's position and responsibilities be established in law. Pauli E. Blomstedt, who took part in the discussion about the responsibility of the architect, considered that since 'the architect designs buildings and town plans only as the entrusted agent of the person who commissions them . . .', it is his duty 'to the best of his ability, to further those interests of his employer that have, with complete confidence, been entrusted to him.' According to this view the architect had no right to pass a moral judgement on the commissions that he accepted. In respect of questions of planning the view held by Blomstedt and adopted by others contained particularly dangerous features: instead of the architect acting in the best interests of the community, he took only the views of the client into consideration and allowed himself to draw up individual plans fully aware that they would upset any large-scale plan for the area.

The significance of this is very difficult to assess since, as planners and advisers to politicians, architects are socially in a key position. After the war, at the same time as the Association of Architects was condemning, for example, the development of the so-called 'white slums', individual architects were taking part in planning them. In 1931 Martti Välikangas criticized the lack of any sense of social ethics displayed by architects:

'The very limited interest in matters of government shown by people with technical qualifications, and their almost total isolation from anything that is to the slightest extent connected with politics, are facts of which we have long been aware . . . The reasons for this stem originally from architects themselves, from our preference for what is convenient, from the now ingrained fear of anything that touches upon the question of responsibility to society and the community . . . The artist who wandered around Italy in his holidays with a sketch book under his arm collecting architectural ideas . . . has become a construction manager . . . nothing gives him the right nor even excuses his continuing to display a negative attitude towards the life and welfare of the community.'

Despite all the talk about social responsibility, functionalism in Finland showed little sign of class consciousness and when it did, it tended to be characteristic of the upper classes by comparison with Sweden and Germany; to say nothing of the Soviet Union. In Finland functionalism was not so obviously the architecture of social reform as it was in the Soviet Union.

At the most the 1930's witnessed a moderate attitude, in certain cases a degree of sympathy, towards socialism and the new order of society. The work of Russian town planners was known and in 1935 Pauli E. Blomstedt published a survey of the new types of towns in the Soviet Union. A characteristic feature in the thinking of town-planners   29 was, in Blomstedt's words, that 'in our environment it is natural that our starting point must continue to be the private initiative in the settlement and development of new areas'. No one demanded a reform in attitude towards social units such as the family. Communism haunted Finland in the 1930's and socially conscious ideas were, as Välikangas has pointed out, generally equated with socialism, which was regarded as undesirable.

The later development of Soviet architecture (during the Stalin era) shocked and disturbed Finnish architects. It led them to abandon even intellectual leftism. There was not a single architect who belonged to the poorer classes, hence their experience of social conflict was wholly theoretical. By abandoning socialism as a means of social development, by consolidating their own social position and by taking the attitude that improvement could be expected in the course of 'natural economic evolution', architects lost touch with politics and this in its turn caused them to lose touch with social measures that were being undertaken.

In accordance with the resolution of C.I.A.M. Blomstedt announced his hope that 'one day legal measures would be taken in Finland to ensure that only architects be allowed to undertake the tasks of building, planning and other architectural projects.' Taking into consideration the number of qualified architects this demand, even today, appears somewhat immoderate. One detects in this the same kind of conceit as appears in Bertel Jung's essay of 1941; in this he expresses his satisfaction that as a result of Lars Sonck's literary controversy (1897) problems of town planning were transferred from engineers to architects. The engineers' subsequent attitude that architects should be artistic experts led to a feeling of inferiority; the engineers have not developed as designers in their own right as Sigurd Frosterus at the beginning of the century and Le Corbusier in the 1920's had hoped.

Nevertheless, the elevation of the architect's position in society also had its good sides. Although functionalism was generally resisted as 'packing-case architecture,' the opposition that architects experienced in Finland was not nearly so great as in most other countries. Moreover Finland did not see in art and architecture the kind of conservatism that was prevalent in the Soviet Union and in Germany after 1930, when the State halted the development of modernism.

Town Planning in the 1930's

The attitude of Finnish architects towards the Soviet Union in the 1930's
30 was not as positive as it might have been. Nevertheless, the work of

the Russian constructivist movement was known in Finland; Ekelund has mentioned that he obtained books very early on about Russian constructivism. Although not much was written about this in Finland, at least not in *Arkkitehti,* it certainly did play a part in shaping Finnish functionalism. The design most reminiscent of the early, heroic spirit of Soviet architecture was Pauli E. Blomstedt's entry, in 1932, for the Kotka Town Hall competition.

Generally the external forms of Blomstedt's work bring to mind Le Corbusier's buildings more sharply than the work of any other Finnish architect. His works always have a powerful form and an animistic expression. Aalto, on the other hand, was nearer Gropius. Blomstedt's architecture betrays a touch of high-flown heaviness in the wall surfaces, which is, however, balanced by the linearality of the whole. Although he died very young, in 1935, Blomstedt designed several important buildings, of which the most significant are the Pohjanhovi Hotel [16], destroyed in the war, the Aulanko Hotel and a small bank in Kotka [17], which is one of the most beautiful buildings of the 1930's — a building that functions like a machine. Perhaps Blomstedt's most important contribution to Finnish architecture is to be found in his numerous writings. Together with Hilding Ekelund, he was a most prolific polemicist. The majority of his writings consider problems related to the Helsinki town plan. It is difficult to find any definite architectural theory in the writings of the 1930's. Like the majority of Le Corbusier's 'theories', they are based more on intuitive observations than on actual research.

Blomstedt provided a form for large-scale functionalist planning. He wrote in favour of the open style of building and drew specimen plans of houses. In the open plan of the 1930's, in which houses were sited compactly in rows, the height of the houses and the distance between them acquired considerable significance. If properly worked out and measured, the spaces between buildings could form safe courtyards — a good example of this is the Olympic Village of 1940 [18] designed by Ekelund and Välikangas.

At the same time as this simple plan with buildings arranged in rows was being advanced, there appeared a more dynamic, free-form plan that had much in common with the *Jugendstil* approach. The connection with the *Jugendstil* is obvious in the Vienna *Werkbundsiedlung.* In Finland Otto-Iivari Meurman was avoiding plans which contained too many straight lines. Aalto also preferred a free form: the Sunila housing estate is fanlike and adapted to the landscape.

On the other hand contemporary foreign influences came together in the rectangular plan with the domestic tradition, the nineteenth- 31 century neo-Classical plan, which in the 1920's had produced the rectangular blocks of the Käpylä garden suburb [2]. Käpylä already contains a feature of the modern open plan idea – the attempt to provide light and plants. The functionalist plan, however, despite its regularity, was felt to be particularly aesthetic: in general it was a question of a graphically beautiful plan. The master plan, which largely replaces visual material with informative material, did not gain acceptance.

The functionalist master plan, which was established in the 1929 C.I.A.M. meeting, later became the subject of severe criticism. According to this plan the various functions and activities of a town should each be located in a different area. At the beginning of the 1930's planners put too much faith in the future development of transport. They thought that cars and other vehicles would increase peoples' range of movement and that therefore the town boundary could be farther from the centre. This attitude also prevailed in Finland and the most important functionalist plans concerned exclusively residential areas.

Le Corbusier was the spiritual father of this new approach to planning. His ideal was the skyscraper city with a population of three million; although it preserved the diagonals of old Paris, the scale was superhuman. Something of this overwhelming scale found expression in the work of Aalto and Blomstedt: their entries for Stockholm's Norrmalm town planning competition (1933) include large blocks of houses set out in straight lines. Those plans would have reshaped the centre of Stockholm as drastically as Le Corbusier's own entry to the competition. Their works were for an architectural Utopia rather than for a social Utopia.

The reform in town planning gained acceptance far more quickly than the reform in building design; a healthy attitude to this problem had already evolved in the 1920's; in 1931 Frosterus wrote that at the beginning of the century planning had been 'a matter of aesthetics, in which the creative eye kept glancing back to the past', whereas the living town had never been an artistic creation. Otto-livari Meurman, one of those who took part in the planning of Käpylä, expressed the pre-functionalist attitude more precisely (1928): 'Planning was not regarded merely as an artistic or traffic movement exercise, rather as an attempt to place the main emphasis on social factors, including, of course, matters of economy and hygiene'.

The basic weakness in the planning for a social Utopia in the 1930's was the confidence in the omnipotent powers of transport. As a result of the belief in the general excellence and desirability of the motor car the planning of communal transport was neglected. Hence Le Corbusier's concept of car traffic driving along raised motorways is more a drama of transport than a search for social contact; nowhere does he present new kinds of vehicles for communal transport.

Homes

The open planning introduced by functionalism brought with it a new type of housing, houses arranged in rows so that none cast its shadow on another, and a new approach to the internal division of the dwelling. In keeping with the spirit of functionalism the internal space was divided up according to the various domestic activities. The free plan evolved in the 1930's provided the solution for the future and has been reproduced in its tens of thousands. But is this standard type really satisfactory?

The free plan of the functionalist dwelling was developed at the beginning of the century in the homes of the more well-to-do; the single roomed dwellings of the poorer people were not an architectural problem. It was thanks to the introduction of more functional furniture and kitchen equipment that the size of the flat could be made smaller and thus came within the reach of the less well-to-do. Here arose the concept of 'minimum existence'. Almost all the leading European architects took part in the creation of the small dwelling; in Finland it occupied the attention of Aalto, Ekelund and Bryggman. Home exhibitions became a favourite type of propaganda. New types of homes were displayed at the Stockholm exhibition of 1930 and in the Finnish one of 1932.

Aalto's Standard block of flats (1927-9), 'Finland's first functionalist building', is a good starting point from which to consider the Finnish approach to housing during the 1930's. At least one of the rooms of the standard dwelling was an all-purpose room, a factor that contradicted functionalist principles. The latest modern building emphasizes the flexible solution, which pre-supposes that the purpose of a room can be varied, and that hence its shape or size cannot be fixed into one single solution. Nevertheless the most common type of dwelling today is still based on the fixed functionalist type and the best solutions are only variants of this type.

The chief object of interest in the 1930's was the flat. Less attention was devoted to the one-family house. This stemmed from economic pressure and urbanization. Aalto did, however, design some houses that differed from the usual type, such as his 'flats without stairs' on a slope in Kauttua (1938-40). In 1932 Hilding Ekelund produced an interesting plan for atrium houses, which is in every respect to be com- 33 pared with what architects are achieving at present: compact small houses as an alternative to the flat.

The most important question of the whole of the first half of the twentieth century was a social one: the solution of the housing shortage. The progressive housing estates for workers of the nineteenth century – the Krupp estate in Essen and Port Sunlight and Bourneville in England – bore fruit in the first two decades of this century in the form of the Garden City principle. Ebenezer Howard's book *Garden Cities of Tomorrow* (1898/1902) influenced not only the design of the Käpylä garden suburb but also functionalist planning as a whole. Through the efforts of Otto-Iivari Meurman, who held the Chair of Planning from 1940, the Garden City principle still exerted its influence on housing areas such as Tapiola in the 1950's.

The Fate of Functionalism

The view that the modernists of the 1930's had considerable scope to put into practice their new ideas gives too positive a picture of what was really happening during this period. Despite Ekelund's assurances to the contrary the new architecture was not widely adopted; the majority of architects continued to design buildings either in the classical style or in some kind of pseudo-modernistic fashion. The ideal form of international architecture – flat-roofed cube houses – ousted the 'traditional' ridge roof to only a very small degree. The argument about 'functionalism and traditionalism' remained bitter on certain points of detail throughout the 1930's and indeed, at a popular level, continues so even today.

The opponents of functionalism included climatic factors in their arguments. The flat roof, a characteristic of the *Bauhaus* and regarded in Germany as a 'Bolshevist device', did not gain so much social significance in Finland. The reason for opposing it was basically aesthetic: the flat roof was not part of the Finnish tradition. From the technical point of view such a roof would not have been an impossibility; such roofs had been constructed at the beginning of the century; moreover, under Finnish climatic conditions it would have had distinct advantages; it would have prevented chunks of frozen snow from falling on passers-by (always a dangerous risk in a Finnish winter) and the snow would also have served as an additional heat insulator.

It was on this manic fear of flat roofs that the far-reaching modernist programme came to grief. If a house has a sloping roof, it is impossible to construct a roof terrace, moreover an internal framework is senseless.

34 Functionalism spread to Finland, but in the form in which it generally

manifested itself clearly deserved its popular name of 'packing-case architecture': white stuccoed houses with stone or board walls and a shed roof disguised as a flat roof. In this form functionalism spread to every part of Finland.

The climate certainly had a limiting influence on structural expression. Only occasionally had the framework of a Finnish building been exposed. Heat insulation problems made it difficult to show the supporting structure on the façade. In Finland functionalism adopted, for the most part, plastic forms: the structure was enclosed within the building or concealed in the wall surface.

Public and industrial buildings displayed the most structurally organized architecture. The gable of the Paimio Sanatorium [7] is perhaps the most expressively articulated. Later in the 1930's Yrjö Lindegren emerged as the purest exponent of constructivism. Apart from many fine entries to competitions, his major project was the Helsinki Olympic Stadium [19], which, together with the sports buildings designed by Hilding Ekelund and Jorma Järvi, was intended for the 1940 Olympics.

After Functionalism

The cancellation of the 1940 Olympics marked the end of the active reforms of the 1930's; the Second World War interrupted the young tradition of modern architecture, despite the fact that the crisis situation caused by the war might have provided a possibility to demonstrate its ability to satisfy the requirements of society. Although the war meant a halt in the development of architecture, it nevertheless provided a creative pause. With ever-limited materials architects had to design emergency accommodation. Perhaps this was even a good counterpoise to the monumental functionalism of the 1930's. At the same time there suddenly appeared a romanticism, stimulated by Swedish influences, which served as a kind of spiritual reaction to the 'hard line' of functionalism. Since there was a danger that cheap materials would produce cheap architecture, even the most rationalist functionalists began to make concessions, and tried to animate wall surfaces with slates or by coarsely finished plaster.

The Second World War put planners in a situation very similar to the one they had known during the First World War. There were, however, two significant differences: on the one hand the new war was far more destructive and on the other it did not bring about so fundamental a change in ethical approach. In 1928 the Swedish architect Sven Markelius pointed out that 'the post-war housing problem and the immense social upheavals of our age have been stimulating factors in the development of contemporary architecture'. After the Second World War the only social innovation was a gradual rise in the standard of living and a transfer of housing production once and for all into the hands of private contractors.

Functionalism had concentrated its attention mainly on housing production, for architects too felt the pressure of industrialization and the movement of population into the towns as a quantitative problem. As the shortage of houses, dating back to the 1920's, grew worse, and the wages of workers rose as a result of industrialization, people began to realise that the old-fashioned brick structure of the *Jugendstil* era had outlived its usefulness. It was felt that the reinforced concrete structure also brought with it an obligation to introduce standardization to home construction.

The Garden City, then, had already established the principle of socially motivated housing production way back in the 1910's. The architecture of Eliel Saarinen's proposal for the development of the Helsinki Suburb, Munkkiniemi-Haaga, which remained for the most part on paper, was coherent and unpretentious, fully in keeping with its English model. In the first half of the 1920's the Käpylä garden suburb [2] was built – the first large-scale housing development to introduce standardization. During the 1930's however, no reinforced concrete factory-built houses were put into production.

Rebuilding in the 1940's concentrated on rural areas more than on towns. It was necessary to re-settle some 400,000 Karelian refugees from the area ceded to the U.S.S.R., and in Lapland, after the destruction wrought by the retreating Germans. Single-family homes rather than blocks of flats were required. The two competitions for the design of small houses held at the beginning of the 1930's were interested in these as holiday residences. Although the terrace-house type was the most developed form of small house, many builders rejected the idea of such close communal living as impracticable.

In 1941 when writing about reconstruction, Aalto emphasised that it was necessary to avoid building barrack-like villages even as an emergency solution, for they would make it completely impossible to improve the situation. On the other hand he admitted the impossibility of building top quality homes of optimum size and fittings immediately. Aalto's proposal was typical of the functionalist mass-production theory in that it arrived at large-scale, rapid production of a primitive 'cell'. The nucleus, once it had relieved immediate needs, could later be extended as and when economic conditions permitted. Right from the very beginning, however, he wanted to standardise in a way that would later allow as wide a range of variation as possible. Aalto's principle was that since 'the ability of that flexible creature, man, to adapt himself to inconsiderate technical limitations is obviously much greater than the ability of technology to adapt itself to the complicated needs of man', standardized houses would create a 'psychological slum' if peoples' varying needs were not taken as the architect's starting-point. While in the United States as a visiting professor Aalto advanced the idea of radical humanism as a counter-balance to extreme American standardization. He illustrated his view with reference to the motor car industry: 'As the number of car models decrease, the products of the architect must do precisely the opposite'.

In 1941 the Finnish Association of Architects set up a Standardization Institute whose early activity was concerned with the development of types of houses suitable for the reconstruction project. Several architects, including Aulis Blomstedt, were invited to be members of the planning group and most of the leading architects offered to help. The activity of the group may indirectly have been responsible for spreading the stereotype, ridge-roofed, single-family house throughout Finland, regarded as the worst step backwards in modern Finnish architecture. It marked the abandonment of functionalist ideals of beauty; the single-family house with its high socles and ridge roof was, moreover, a poor imitation of the traditional low farmhouse.

On the other hand, an observer not bound by aesthetic norms might well regard this type of house, which definitely reflected popular taste, as super-functionalist, in so far as requirements and possibilities were concerned. The houses could be built by self-taught carpenters, of whom there was no shortage, and they used the easiest obtainable material, wooden planks. The carpenter-builder had no wish to imitate 'architecture' which he regarded as irrational aestheticism. Aesthetic factors had to yield to 'economic' requirements; hence in this respect the single-family house provides the best illustration of the various hierarchies of functionalism. The most important improvement in this field is the low, cellarless, single-family house, similar in style to the old farmhouse, which came into fashion at the end of the 1950's and blends best with the natural background.

It is most important to remember that the single-family house was not merely an emergency solution even then. It had already become clear in the 1930's that there was a need to modify some of the severe stylistic features of functionalism such as the flat roof, which gave a building a box-like appearance. In Sweden, whose old cultural tradition gave rise to different standards of taste, the requirements of domestic comfort had, at an early stage, displaced the harsh Corbusian line. In Finland there were also early signs of rejection – a conflict arose 37 between ideology and the traditional approach to comfort. Erik Bryggman became the exponent of Swedish standards of taste ('Swedish grace') in Finland. The villa he designed at Kuusisto (1941) [20] is both the purest and most pleasing example of the romantic architecture of the 1940's. The romantic forms of the chapel he designed in Turku (1940) also reveal decorative details characteristic of functionalism. The Turku church is a far less impressive work for a transitional period than the chapel Bryggman built ten years earlier at Parainen: the barren harsh classicism of the latter had contained the promise of a new idealism.

The change, which can with good reason be regarded as a betrayal of the earlier ideas, was general. Although we must bear in mind the difficulties of obtaining materials, the romantic tendency is obvious, whether one sees it as a reaction to functionalism or as caused by the war. Every architect, including Aalto, Lindegren, Aulis Blomstedt and Viljo Revell, designed ridge-roofed buildings, whose porches or chimneys were decorated by 'artistically' placed slates. The most romantic feature was the log sauna [22], a consciously nostalgic object, in which the bathing ritual involved the presence of traditional national style.

In 1946 Nils Erik Wickberg, professor of the history of architecture, pointed with mixed feelings to the increasingly frequent attempts to modify functionalism by flavouring it with traditional, historical features.

'Whatever one thinks of Le Corbusier, he did represent a logical line, a conviction, and, like the bird at daybreak, he announced the "dawning of a new era".'

The abandonment of this romantic interlude occurred gradually as a result of internal necessity, but it was not easy. It was only to be expected that popular opinion, which had so quickly accustomed itself to the romantic line, would be all the more resistant to functionalist forms. Nevertheless modern reinforced concrete architecture had been born, and its existence could not indefinitely be concealed behind an archaic skin. Yrjö Lindegren, who designed the Olympic Stadium, took a cautious step in this direction in his Helsinki Snake Building *(Käärmetalo* 1951) [23], whose sinuous form, despite rationalist precepts such as the need to let in light and retain a view, was romantically variable, while its flat roof and detail of form were rooted in functionalism. This return was far more obvious in the building of the Industrial Centre *(Teollisuuskeskus* 1952) [30] designed by Viljo Revell and Keijo Petäjä. The form of the whole is reminiscent of Le Corbusier, the simple strip façade is lively but proportionally harmonious.

38   On the whole the architecture of the 1950's continued the func-

tionalist tradition. The ideology of functionalism survived because it was the general ideology of modern architecture, whereas in the 1930's it had been more a contemporary shape than an ideology. It is important to remember this distinction when talking of 'functionalism', which can refer to an ideology or a historical period. In the 1950's modern architecture was reborn, and in its choice of materials and styles, far more varied and prolific than the architecture of the 1930's.

Alvar Aalto

The most obvious change brought by the 1950's was Aalto's adoption of red brick. In 1952 the manifesto of the new era, the Säynätsalo Town Hall [25], was completed. The composition is richer throughout, the interweaving of themes more obvious than in the works of the 1930's. A new feature is intimacy; the natural background shares more organically in the overall composition. In Säynätsalo Aalto has given up his axialism and the internal drama corresponds to the external drama. In some respects the building calls to mind Aalto's suggestion for the Tallinn Museum [9], although the monumentality of the earlier work has been replaced by an archaic, romantic randomness. A new feature, which is repeated in later buildings, is the relationship between their dominating and 'neutral' parts; in many public buildings the dominating hall space becomes an outward-looking characteristic.

In considering Aalto's skill in handling space it becomes obvious that he preferred enclosed, evenly limited space — despite the fact that the shape of a hall often depended on the nature of the undertaking. It can be established that Aalto did not aim at the same kind of open, structural architecture as, for example, Mies van der Rohe. The construction of the Paimio Sanatorium has no place in this post-war architecture. Aalto's critical attitude to 'technological architecture', i.e. constructivism, emerges from his writing about people as the focal point of architecture and the importance of humanism in the process of planning. One is justified in regarding his buildings as an answer to this humanitarian requirement. Yet on the other hand Aalto did not clearly define the kind of architecture he regarded as inhuman. Could this perhaps include the steel and glass architecture of Mies van der Rohe?

Aalto's buildings frequently contain areas that form simultaneously both external and internal spaces; examples of this are the marbled court of the Steel Federation building in Helsinki *(Rautatalo)* [26] and the large staircase hall of the University of Jyväskylä. The ceiling lights first used in the Viipuri Library diminish the effects of internal space. 39

Several interiors contain features which create the same illusion, e.g. the gallery in the New York pavilion. Writers on architecture see some of the inspiration for Aalto's freely formed spaces in the lake and island scenery of the Finnish countryside. It is clear that these hall areas are specimens of the architect's virtuosity and hence less appropriate for adoption by other architects than architecture aimed at an anonymous constructivism. Aalto's forms are regarded as national in the same way as Eliel Saarinen's national-romantic architecture. In so far as national consciousness is concerned, the birth of this myth has been fruitful and not particularly dangerous, since the position of the 'maestro' has been balanced by the existence of a large number of other good architects.

Since the 1950's Aalto has obtained increasingly important commissions, some of them as the result of competitions. For many public buildings, such as the National Pensions Institute in Helsinki (*Kansaneläkelaitos,* 1956) [31], Aalto has designed even the smallest details including furniture and lighting. The Helsinki House of Culture [27] and the church at Vuoksenniska (1958) are the best examples of Aalto's skill at forming large, free-formed internal spaces. His proposal for the opera house at Essen in Germany, in which the foyer and the auditorium opened out like a baroque hall surrounded by galleries one on top of the other, has not been built. Many of Aalto's entries to competitions abroad met the same fate. The Aalborg Museum of the Arts in Denmark, reminiscent of Aalto's plans for the Tallinn Museum, was neglected for many years before it was finally built. His entry to the competition for the Vienna Congress Hall was one of his structurally bolder plans; the wide, free-form hall area would have had a ceiling hanging from steel wires.

New Rationalism

The leading representative of constructivism in Finland was Viljo Revell, who died in 1964. He was one of the architects involved in the design of Helsinki's first functionalist building, the Glass Palace *(Lasipalatsi)* [15], completed in 1935. After the war his architecture became characterized by a horizontalism which, on the one hand, may derive from functionalism while, on the other, has been explained as symbolic of the view of the sea from his birthplace (Vaasa). Revell was in any case inclined towards the large-scale, which was appropriate in his solutions for such monumental constructions in the New World as Toronto Town Hall or the Buenos Aires Peugeot Building (a competition project in 1962), but alien on the smaller scale of the Finnish town. His plans for

large sectors of Finnish towns in his later years cut across the traditional land divisions of the area; his designs for the centre of Vaasa and the Helsinki City Centre complex seem to dwarf the surrounding old buildings.

The design for Toronto Town Hall was an attempt to discover a new monumentalism, a powerful image, to balance the huge business buildings in the town. The building turns its back on the town in an almost escapist gesture. In the construction stage Revell had to make certain structural compromises, which lessened the strict principles of the original design.

Revell took part in the attempt to industrialize the construction of houses. In 1954 a block of flats constructed entirely of prefabricated reinforced concrete parts was completed in Tapiola; the building, as was common in Revell's flats, had a highly systematical basic plan. Nevertheless his approach did not succeed in competition with projects that employed larger prefabricated parts. Revell later designed the blocks of flats along Kaskenkaataja Road [34], whose reinforced concrete walls and floors, cast on the spot, are visible in the façade and create a beautiful yet modest sight.

Revell's approach to his work was exceptional in that he designed each of his buildings in partnership with one of the architects in his office. Revell's 'academy' produced such men as Osmo Sipari, Keijo Petäjä, Martti Jaatinen, Osmo Lappo, Bengt Lundsten and others, who were all subsequently to continue the rationalist line.

Another of Aalto's 'pupils' of the 1930's, Aarne Ervi, also investigated the possibilities of prefabricated structures which he used, for example, in the Institute Building of the University of Helsinki (1951). The new buildings of the University of Turku were constructed at almost the same time as Aalto's campus at the University of Jyväskylä; whereas Aalto located his buildings as the continuation of a wooded ridge, Ervi, planning in an urban environment in Turku, sited the faculty buildings in a compact rectangular group around a courtyard of an optimum size. Although the simplicity of Ervi's architecture is sometimes monotonous, it has, in its overall effect, preserved something of the spirit of the 1930's.

Revell and Ervi have departed considerably from Aalto's line. Aalto's obvious leading position has inspired other architects to seek other means of expression – a measure that has done much to stimulate the Finnish architectural scene. Heikki Siren and Veli Paatela, for example, who at one stage were both clearly influenced by Aalto's use of bricks, have established their own line. Imitators of Aalto outside Finland are only found in Denmark and Italy, where Aalto has a large number of adherents.

41

Aulis Blomstedt has often been seen as a contrast to Alvar Aalto. Whereas the latter refuses to develop any standard modules in his works, Blomstedt has, since the 1930's, devoted himself to exploring modular patterns and in a more general form, harmonical patterns. Of all the Finnish architects he has taken the most serious interest in the challenge of industry and providing for mass production. Large numbers cause a production problem to which the solution is the industrial production of buildings. However there is a lack of any international standardization system or instrument of coordination. As a means of creating such an instrument Aulis Blomstedt attempted, like Le Corbusier and Ehrenkrantz before him, to unite factors that did not cohere easily; the ideal numerical relationship pattern and a practically feasible system of measurements. He settled on the Canon sixty, which, being based on whole numbers, is more flexible than Le Corbusier's irrational relationship pattern. Although the series of numbers looks simple, it makes possible many kinds of dimensional patterns.

Both Pauli E. Blomstedt and his brother Aulis frequently took part in competitions during the 1930's; the latter, however, did not begin to build his more important works until the beginning of the 1950's. As one of the leading professors of architecture from 1958 until 1966 he imparted both direction and substance to the rationalism of the younger generation and in the 1950's steered architecture away from uninspired realism towards more idealist goals. Aulis Blomstedt is an enormously prolific essayist who turns his penetrating analytical mind to the essence and basic themes of architecture, the relationship between architecture and nature, housing problems, and many others.

Although Aulis Blomstedt's extraordinary proposal for an aluminium building in 1954 was a unique open, constructivist project, he nevertheless showed the younger generation of architects the way to the influence of Le Corbusier and Mies van der Rohe. At the beginning of the 1960's Finnish architecture found itself, in many respects, in the same ideological position as in 1927. Architects were faced with a similar social situation, the same trend of modernism and a similar stylistic crisis. The younger architects formed new links with functionalism. Le Corbusier's influence has been most obvious during the present decade in the works of Aarno Ruusuvuori; from these a new, contemporary rationalism has gradually evolved.

Ruusuvuori, who was appointed professor of architecture in 1963, brings a brilliant sense of form to the use of simple materials; reinforced concrete, steel and glass. Ruusuvuori's office competes with Aalto's for the design of Finland's most beautiful detail. Ruusuvuori's choice of materials is, however, more stratified. His office produces primitive architecture, of the kind which British critics call 'brutalism'. Surprisingly, Ruusuvuori's internationalism is among the most pleasing phenomena of Finnish architecture: it demonstrates that in abstract rationalism Finnish architecture has reached an international standard.

New Romanticism?

Finnish architecture is becoming less and less an isolated phenomenon. The numerous professional journals quickly disseminate new ideas to an international audience and thus projects evolved in Finland very soon come to the attention of architects around the world. The universality of architecture has itself given birth to various new national movements. In Finland the architecture of Reima Pietilä is the most obvious example.

National traits are found in Aalto's work in certain local variations from the mainstream of international architecture. Pietilä, on the contrary, seems to be striving to avoid international rationalism. Although one does not need to see any typical Finnish traits, as such, in his architecture, it is nevertheless especially Finnish in its unconcerned individuality. If Aalto is the idealist who wants to bring a warm humanity to international rationalism, then Pietilä is the anarchist who wants to avoid generally approved architectural norms.

In the 1960's many Finnish architects have felt great concern for the question of an architectural style: functionalistic modernism is labelled nostalgic, international constructivism is regarded as alien and no-one wants to imitate Aalto's highly personal architecture. Pietilä can be compared to Lars Sonck; the return to old-fashioned materials and the structural forms to which they were best suited was a determined personal decision, taken at the turn of the century when the secure image of architecture was obscured by structural and social problems. The creation of a new style served as a symbolic gesture and Sonck's buildings were so powerful in character that they were rarely criticized on strictly architectural grounds.

The student union of the Institute of Technology, *Dipoli* (1966) [45], is regarded as an example of contemporary Finnish symbolic architecture. *Dipoli* takes as its starting point the established architectural form of the former student union, a granite building dating from 1903 and containing cave-like spaces. The same technique was used to give *Dipoli* the national romantic mood of the old building.

Pietilä's Kaleva Church in Tampere (1966) [54] is reminiscent of Aalto's forest pavilion of 1938 [11] in that a free-formed space is enclosed by a series of vertical features and the internal form is reflected 43 in the building's exterior. The Kaleva Church, with its cathedral dimensions, is regarded as the most church-like of modern Finnish churches. Controversy over the external appearance of churches was not limited to the 1930's; in the 1950's a professor of architecture, Nils Erik Wickberg, had to explain the fundamentals of ecclesiastical architecture to members of the clergy. He regarded the ambiguity of the Lutheran liturgy as one of the reasons why the clergy themselves were unable to define the requirements of a modern church and why they demanded that churches should be 'traditional' in appearance, i.e. like the medieval stone churches built before the Reformation.

Wickberg's criticism seems to have had an immediate effect. Local church councils found it profitable to employ bold modernist designs, numerous competitions were organized and the architects who participated in church planning – not always believers themselves – designed architecturally interesting buildings in which the religious mood has not always been achieved with verticalism. It is against this background that Pietilä's church in Tampere is church-like in the traditional 'Gothic' sense, an effect achieved through the most modern architectural devices.

Nevertheless, Pietilä's unique free forms are not a nationally isolated phenomena. They are related to the old 'anarchist' tradition best known through the work of the German, Hans Scharoun. The only nationalist feature in *Dipoli* is the conscious attempt to make it an extension of the natural background.

The Crisis of Urbanism

Urbanization is new to Finland. Nature is still powerful and mystical and architecture often reflects a primitive attitude towards nature and a kind of nature mysticism. At the beginning of the century national romanticism was characterized by the forest; its details depicted bears, squirrels, conifers. Modern architecture reflects various features. As previously noted, the horizontality of the buildings of Viljo Revell, who was a keen yachtsman, has been seen as symbolizing the open seascape seen from Vaasa, his birthplace. Reima Pietilä's student building at *Dipoli* is based on the idea that it is an extension of the natural background both in its external form and in the boulders retained inside the building.

The rationalists of the 1930's were furthest from nature mysticism; their buildings were in conscious contrast to nature, indeed they thought that both architecture and nature profited from this clearly defined ideological and plastic division. The revival of interest in the natural background during the 1940's followed in the wake of the intellectual architecture of the previous decade and led to the rejection of the simple functionalist approach to planning. A free plan evolved, which was different from the dynamically controlled, all-powerful plan favoured by *Art Nouveau*. This kind of area planning spread to Finland in the 1950's; a typical example of its influence is the first part of Tapiola on which work started in 1952.

This plan — or anti-plan — has its own history. Otto-Iivari Meurman had drawn up a plan to use the area for small houses; his plan was a non-urban, meandering scheme which would have been suitable for an estate of single-family houses. When the area was bought by the *Asuntosäätiö* (Housing Foundation) building society, the contractor responsible for Tapiola, there was no time to revise the plan to accommodate blocks of flats and rows of terraced houses. From this 'accident' there evolved a new ideology which had affinities with, for example, contemporary planning in Sweden. Tapiola [32-40] became an important prototype which was publicized as a garden suburb, although it is in fact a sparsely-built forest town. The houses are situated in small groups, planned by different architects, without any unifying overall plan. Although the planning of first stages of Tapiola won many adherents, the planning of the subsequent areas moved towards a greater degree of compactness and urbanization. The planning reveals in the grouping of buildings a return to a systematic approach, although the groups continued to be sited separately in wooded areas. Physical geography did not prove to be an obstacle, on the contrary the taller buildings were placed on the highest points and green fields between the clumps of forest were left untouched as recreational areas.

The free-form forest town can be regarded as an anarchist stand against everything that planning historically stands for; it is not the same thing as the organically evolved medieval town. Since the Second World War, Finland has been seen as a pioneer in social planning and Tapiola has been the model for success in this field. However, it was later observed that proximity to nature does not entirely compensate for the accompanying deprivations of urban conveniences. Where distances are too great to be covered on foot, the increase in the number of cars puts an end to idealism: the road system has proved inadequate, motor traffic and pedestrians criss-cross dangerously.

It is only in the 60's that a new, compact type of plan has evolved. Concentration provides the best opportunity for separating vehicular and pedestrian traffic. The new plans drawn up in this spirit diverge from the common functionalist pattern in that the groups of houses form half-closed blocks and the open spaces begin more and more to 45 resemble the streets of old towns. This presupposes that motor traffic is restricted to main roads around the area and that the spaces within the area are left as safe thoroughfares even for children. In Finland as elsewhere, the use of the private car has become the most important factor in social planning and it has been assumed, in placing housing areas far from the centre of towns, that every family will one day own a car. Transport would not have been so important a factor had housing areas originally been planned economically and perhaps administratively, as self-sufficient units.

Harto Helpinen is the only planner to suggest the ideal town plan from which the car would be wholly excluded (in a project for his degree). His town plan contains a centre and a large number of small groups of housing; traffic is conveyed between the accommodation areas and the centre by fast 'horizontal lifts'. There has in fact been very little idealist town planning since the seventeenth and eighteenth centuries. Nowadays the interest of planners is shifting from the aesthetic problems of planning to social planning, in which the important role of abstract, theoretical material requires the architect to collaborate with experts from other fields. In place of the old norms of town planning it has become necessary to take into consideration people's real needs when planning housing areas.

The move from the plastically formed to the systematic plan is symbolized by a return to the neutral square plan. The rectangular town plan has a long tradition in Finland, from the regular layouts of the seventeenth century through the neo-Classical town plan of the nineteenth century down to Käpylä in the 1920's. The best example of the new town plan is Bengt Lundsten's design for the Kortepohja district of Jyväskylä [57] in which the size of the housing blocks corresponds to the historical size of the town's blocks; the traditional scale is also reflected in the height of the houses.

In the course of rebuilding old towns, traffic demands, requiring the widening of streets, have often led to the destruction of the historical town plan. This has occurred in Turku to Carl Ludwig Engel's magnificent garden town plan. In some cases coherent town planning has saved irreplaceable town environments, as, for example, in Olli Kivinen's plan for Hamina which preserved the octagonal shape of the town dating from the beginning of the eighteenth century and provided a new centre next to it.

Symbolically the most important design project since the beginning of the century has been the centre of Helsinki. In addition to the unique Empire Style centre there has long been a need for a modern, efficient

business and cultural centre. Eliel Saarinen's plan for Greater Helsinki

(1918) was the most radical of several suggestions: it proposed a densely-built central axis running north from the old city. Planning schemes in the 1930's were still based on Saarinen's proposal, although not one of them was ever actually realised. In 1948 another competition was held to find a plan for the area, but no satisfactory results were obtained. Subsequently Yrjö Lindegren and his assistant Erik Kråkström were commissioned to produce a plan, which they completed in 1953. Their proposal was shelved and after Lindegren's death the commission was given to Alvar Aalto, whose suggestions were accepted as the basis for a detailed plan.

In Aalto's plan [50] the symbolically most important factor is the cultural centre placed alongside Töölö Bay, of which the concert and congress building will be put up first. The overall plan also embraces the central traffic system, the expansion of the business area and the bus station. Although the plan in the form put forward by Aalto appears more or less complete, it will nevertheless require considerable research into detail, since the new centre is to be dovetailed into the overall town plan. There is therefore still a long time to wait before the project will be realised in its entirety.

Housing Determines the Occupant's Way of Life

The functionalist solution to the problem of housing received a setback through the postwar building producing programme and all inspired features such as internal galleries were rejected. On the other hand the basic functional division of rooms was retained, for example the typical living room, cannot be used as a study or bedroom because it is not possible to isolate it from the other rooms. In the extensive post-war housing programme people no longer spoke of solving the housing problem in the same idealistic tone as they had in the 1930's. On the contrary, the standards stipulated by the State in the homes for which it was lending the money, restricted individual planners; these standards made no positive contribution to improving architectural quality, indeed they limited it.

The question of building homes for the working classes was neglected, with the result that in prevailing market conditions the less well-to-do had to be satisfied with the smallest possible accommodation. Since home-production in Finland is founded almost exclusively on the principle of private ownership, the construction of one-roomed flats was the most profitable from the contractor's point of view. The 'improvement' of the Kallio residential district of Helsinki is the most striking example of this practice. Even at the time of building the houses gained 47 the reputation of being a 'white slum': from the outside they look modern and elegant.

The abandonment of ideology is clearly revealed in a comparison of these unofficial workers' homes with those built at Käpylä and Vallila during the socially enlightened 1920's. Instead of each flat being used as a separate residence, these one-roomed flats were occupied by young couples with or without children. Local authorities sold the land to the highest bidder irrespective of his motive. Socially, architects have been members of the upper class and have transmitted their own aesthetic values into the buildings they were designing; they did not develop various factors that might have had an immediately beneficial effect, such as standardization to reduce costs. This lack of a positive approach to standardization has led the less confident architects to restrict their approach to the architectural forms and effects they acquired as students; simple rationalism has been replaced by a stylistic form, – for example, the load-bearing brick wall is frequently disguised from the outside as a functionalist wall with strip windows.

Private building contractors have also been reluctant to further universally applicable standards. The lower costs that followed from the limited standardization that did take place benefitted the builder not the customer. The same kind of situation is to be found in many other countries. 1968, however, saw in Finland the beginning of a research project initiated by the Housing Commission and intended to modernise the production of prefabricated buildings. This implies first and foremost, modernization of the basic system of modular standards.

The most common type of solution for the flat, handed down from the functionalist period, has a decisive effect on the occupants' way of life. Architecturally the best flats result from attempts to break away from this conventional type and provide the concept of housing with a new intellectual content. Since the 1930's Aalto has produced many interesting solutions to housing projects, e.g. the Sunila housing estate and the house at Kauttua. Aalto's house at the Berlin *Interbau* exhibition (1957) contained a living room in the style of the traditional Finnish farmhouse; it provided the focal point of the house, on to which all the other rooms opened.

Aulis Blomstedt likewise designed several kinds of house. Of particular importance is his design for a housing exhibition, *Citadelli,* which takes as its starting point the relationship between the home and surrounding natural background – contrary to the usual Finnish solution of the one-family house whose surrounding yard or garden provides no privacy whatsoever if one leaves the house. In Blomstedt's design, on the contrary, the whole of the house including the recreation area and garden is enclosed on two levels within the main walls. Finns are less accustomed than, for example, the peoples of Central Europe, to living in towns, which leads to certain emotional problems in using outside areas. They avoid doing things in the yard for fear that neighbours will stare, *yet because of the neighbours* they do not surround themselves with fences or stone walls. The Finns are still very close to that point in the past when everyone lived in rural conditions free from the gaze of immediate neighbours. On the other hand the custom in smaller towns of surrounding the yard with a tall plank fence has been forgotten. Hence the Finn finds it difficult to adapt to life in a terraced house; and he finds it equally difficult to adopt the most recent type of one-family dwelling, the atrium house, which is built around the yard or garden. The most fruitful development of the atrium house is found in Pentti Ahola's Hakalehto estate [38], where the houses for the main part open on to their own yards or gardens.

Structuralism

Modern architecture shows the victory of rationality, for it has finally achieved the aim towards which architects have worked since the beginning of this century. It has freed itself of ornamentation and the classical tradition that ornamentation represented. The new construction has evolved into a new architecture. Nevertheless even modern architecture has its own 'style' functionalism rooted in a harmonious stylistic whole. In the 1940's and 1950's architects strove to free themselves from functionalist forms, yet failed to discover a distinct form of expression of their own. The 60's have displayed a pluralism with many new parallel stylistic forms, each of which is a rational result within its own terms of reference.

Functionalist architects often made reinforced concrete serve their own ends. Compared to steel, which generally requires a constructivist structure (columns and girders), concrete can be cast into almost any shape. Its flexibility has led to a wide variety of modern reinforced concrete architecture — from the shells of Felix Candela to Japanese mock-constructivism. The exposed reinforced concrete frame has been a rarity in Finland, probably because of the need for heat insulation. The Kråkström-Mikkola-Pallasmaa design for the Puotila school [57] is a typical solution for the Finnish climate; the articulated reinforced concrete frame had to be covered externally by thin insulating material and a skin of sheet metal.

Finland does, however, possess a traditional material which can serve both as a load-bearing frame and as insulating material: wood.

The present decade has seen the birth of wood constructivism reminiscent of traditional Japanese wood architecture [59]. The products of this new architecture are small, one-family houses [60] and summer houses [61], and have been designed by the youngest generation of architects. In addition to its points of contact with Japanese architecture, this use of wood naturally recalls the steel constructivism of Mies van der Rohe, since it automatically presupposes an open-plan design.

Emotional factors have occupied a more important role in Finnish architecture than the development of building technology. Selim A. Lindqvist's early reinforced concrete architecture and Alvar Aalto's investigations into the flexibility of wood have been followed by only a few technical innovations. Obviously a country in the process of industrialization cannot produce the kind of revolutionary structural technology of a Buckminster Fuller or a Frei Otto. Building techniques are out-dated, if only because contractors in the private building sector have not thought it worthwhile to carry out large-scale basic planning. This explains why, for example, Aulis Blomstedt's pioneer dimensional research has remained an expression of personal idealism and has had no practical application in the building industry. Other countries, however, are only in the process of developing universally applicable standards and it is possible that these private projects will one day be utilized to set up international building standards.

The progress of industrial architecture, which has been left to the initiative of private enterprise, is most obvious in small buildings. Since the industrialized prefabrication of blocks of flats has taken the design of building units out of the hands of architects, the planners' own contribution has sufficed for small subjects without the expenditure of large sums on research. Kaija and Heikki Siren and Aarno Ruusuvuori have, among others, designed one-family houses for industrialized prefabrication [59]. The most attractive designs are the summer houses by Kristian Gullichsen and Juhani Pallasmaa, in which the unit size is 225 cm [63].

The broader, varying units of these new types of building have begun to become known as structuralist architecture. The use of this term reveals the recognition that individual buildings are parts of a wider context. Every single town obviously has all kinds of different structures; as nowadays it has become increasingly necessary to plan in advance whole towns or parts of them, social structures, communication structures, installation structures, etc., all have to be taken into consideration. Serge Chermayeff and Christopher Alexander in the United States have won recognition for their work in developing the techniques of structuralization. They have taken as their starting point the relationship between the individual and the community, a sociological approach, and attempted to take into consideration the possibilities of contact between people as well as all the other features of a full and contented life.

In Finland, structuralism has been criticized by the older generation of architects. Though social planning has developed from two polarized units, the individual and the community, the individual's needs have only been seen in terms of housing, whereas the overall plan for an area has been developed as a plastic whole. Hence even architects' interest in such medial forms as the collective or service building has been limited.

By concentrating mainly on the questions of community planning and not on human contacts, architects have been able to function as independent planners. It is only recently that people have realised the inevitability and necessity of collaboration in solving the 'invisible' functions of a community. The idea of teamwork was at first strongly opposed by architects, and even Aalto confessed to a certain foreboding. A good example of planning which, thanks to teamwork, was able to take social structures into consideration, is Bengt Lundsten's design for Kortepohja [57].

The change in attitude of the younger generation of architects from problems of architecture to problems of human relations may, thanks to structuralist thinking, become permanent, and thus lead to a different kind of architecture altogether – to basic frameworks with variable functions, to an open, flexible architecture.

Captions

1   SELIM A. LINDQVIST, Suvilahti power station, Helsinki 1908-13. A mature pioneer work of Finnish concrete constructivism comparable to Auguste Perret's early concrete buildings. The load-bearing columns are clearly visible.

2   MARTTI VÄLIKANGAS and others, Käpylä Garden Suburb, Helsinki 1920-5. A fine synthesis of the British garden city principle (Ebenezer Howard) and Finnish architectural tradition. The overall area layout differs from the type favoured by the exponents of the British and Continental *Art Nouveau* movement. It is based on rectangular blocks and as such represents the planning tradition of seventeenth-century Finland. Although the houses themselves are reminiscent of Ostrobothnian farm houses, they are in fact characterized by a high degree of structural standardization. Considering that they were intended to be working-class dwellings, they are surprisingly spacious.

3   ALVAR AALTO, Workers' Club House, Jyväskylä 1925. One of Aalto's earlier works, it combines the large, blank walls popular in the 1920's with a colonnade theme that anticipates functionalist constructivism. The architectural duality is demanded by the building's function: the upper floor is a hall for meetings and private parties, while the ground floor, with its large window areas opening on to the street, houses restaurant premises.

4   SIGURD FROSTERUS, Stockmann department store, Helsinki 1924-30. The competition to find a design for the store took place in 1916, almost ten years before work on the store began. Hence the emphatically vertical structuralism represents a style typical of the 1910's. In commercial buildings and banks it continued to be used throughout the following decade.

5   OIVA KALLIO, Pohja Insurance Co. Building, Helsinki 1930. The first building in the capital to be built with the strip windows favoured by the functionalist school. The plentiful ornamentation, however, shows that Kallio's ideas were, to a large extent, typical of the 1920's.

6   ALVAR AALTO, Offices of the newspaper *Turun Sanomat,* Turku 1929. The first building in Finland to display all the characteristics of functionalism: a reinforced concrete frame, strip windows and a roof garden.

7   ALVAR AALTO, Tuberculosis Sanatorium, Paimio 1929-33. Aalto's boldest interpretation of the 'new architecture', a building that won international fame as a model of functionalism. The sanatorium's design was first drafted for an architectural competition held in 1928. When it was decided to adopt his proposal, Aalto redesigned every detail of the sanatorium including even furniture and sanitation units.

8   ALVAR AALTO, Public library, Viipuri (now part of the U.S.S.R.) 1930-5. Aalto's design for the Viipuri library competition was prepared in 1927 and was wholly in keeping with the classicism of the 1920's. Evidence of this remained in many aspects of the finished building even though every detail was redesigned in the functionalist idiom. The heavy, blank wall surfaces served the special function of reducing noise, a factor of paramount importance for a library. Aalto's original solution of the lighting problem initiated a style that became a distinctive feature of his later work: natural light comes in through round openings in the ceiling designed to ensure even distribution of light. The lecture hall's undulating ceiling was an accoustic innovation of great importance and was probably the earliest example of Aalto's 'free line' technique.

9   ALVAR AALTO, Competition project for the Tallinn (Estonia) Museum of Art, 1936. This design incorporated the principles that were demonstrated so brilliantly in the Viipuri Library. At the same time, however, the design also represents a constructivist, open functionalism.

10   ALVAR AALTO, Finnish pavilion at the New York World Fair 1939. The pavilion introduced to the New World Aalto's use of free form and wood. Although his contribution was limited to the interior design of the finished building, Aalto used an all-embracing solution to create a dynamic space, a solution which was the starting point for his later approach to problems of space.   53

11   ALVAR AALTO, Pavilion at the Lapua Forestry Exhibition, 1938. This light, temporary building allowed the complete integration of interior and exterior. The upright tree trunks made it possible to mould the walls into any shape required.

12   ALVAR AALTO, Glass vases, about 1938. Aalto's amoeba shape was a personal response to the rigidity of functionalism. It stemmed from a sensitive and intuitive artist's experiment with shapes. Aalto not only expressed these in glass, but also in buildings and furniture.

13   ALVAR AALTO, Sunila cellulose factory, Karhula 1936-9 and 1954. The Sunila project was Aalto's largest undertaking during the 1930's. It consists of a factory and an employees' housing estate. Aalto showed extraordinary skill in translating the production process into a series of cubist shapes. The housing estate is sited on a wooded slope and laid out in a fan pattern. He attempted to give each flat its own identity by building the three-storied blocks into the side of a slope, thus allowing each flat to have its own outside entrance.

14   ERKKI HUTTUNEN, SOK (co-operative organization) factory and warehouse, Helsinki 1937. The reinforced concrete frame of the functionalist structure was particularly suited to industrial buildings.

15   NIILO KOKKO, VILJO REVELL, HEIMO RIIHIMÄKI, Glass Palace, Helsinki 1935. Project designed by three architecture students and the first purely functionalist building to be erected in Helsinki.

16   PAULI E. BLOMSTEDT, Pohjanhovi Hotel, Rovaniemi 1935. Typical of Blomstedt's powerful, somewhat heavy functionalism, which was clearly influenced by Le Corbusier's work. The hotel was destroyed towards the end of the Second World War.

17   PAULI E. BLOMSTEDT, Bank building, Kotka 1935. One of the finest examples of Finnish functionalism. The ground plan and section form a brilliant three dimensional 'machine'. The board-room is sited on the inside gallery.

18   HILDING EKELUND & MARTTI VÄLIKANGAS, Olympic Village, Helsinki 1940. Like the Stadium, constructed for the 1940 Olympic Games which were cancelled because of the outbreak of war. Of the large-scale area developments during the 1930's the Olympic Village is, after the Sunila project, the largest and best designed.

The blocks of flats are simple and built in straight rows according to functionalist principles. The gaps between the blocks are large enough to form pleasant recreational areas.

19 YRJÖ LINDEGREN & TOIVO JÄNTTI, Olympic Stadium, Helsinki 1934-40. Like the Paimio Sanatorium the Stadium is one of the manifestations of the 'white architecture' of the 1930's. The grandstand was later extended. A wooden addition was built for the 1952 Olympics and office premises were later built beneath the Stadium. These additions, unfortunately, spoil the original concept.

20 GUNNAR TAUCHER, Bonded warehouse, Helsinki 1937. Reveals the high standard of Helsinki municipal architecture. Under the direction of Gunnar Taucher, senior architect of the City of Helsinki, many leading architects shared in the planning of municipal buildings during the 1920's. Among them were Pauli E. Blomstedt, Aarne Hytönen and Risto-Veikko Luukkonen of whom the last two assisted Taucher in designing the bonded warehouse.

21 ERIK BRYGGMAN, Private house, Kuusisto 1941. One of the most uncompromising examples of the romantic tendency of the 1940's of which Bryggman was a leading exponent. Characteristic features include plaster surfaces, stone slabs, cane furniture and large potted plants.

22 AULIS BLOMSTEDT, Sauna, Evitskog 1946. Sauna is an old Finnish custom, an idyll which allows the architect to escape to a romantic traditionalism. Just as the Japanese tea room was created for the tea ceremony so the log sauna was evolved for the ritual of cleansing and invigorating oneself both physically and mentally.

23 YRJÖ LINDEGREN, Käärmetalo, flats, Helsinki 1951. Instead of placing a single long building the length of a site or a row of several buildings at right angles to the length of the site, Lindegren designed a long, winding line, thus ensuring maximum variety in outward perspective. Inside the building the curving structure can be noticed only in the stair halls, kitchens and bathrooms. The living rooms are the normal rectangular shape.

24 AULIS BLOMSTEDT, Flats for invalids, Turku 1951. The first of many blocks of flats designed by Blomstedt. His basic layout has changed little, although he has altered the articulation of the façade from the wholly horizontal to a neutral grid (cf. 33 and 35). 55

Together with Lindegren's Käärmetalo, this building is one of the earliest examples of the return to more rational lines after the romanticism of the 1940's.

25 ALVAR AALTO, Säynätsalo Town Hall, 1952. In Aalto's hands romanticism received a totally new significance and meaning. It was no longer a superficial idiosyncrasy but expressed a sense of humanity in scale and form. The Town Hall is a satisfying combination of monumentalism demanded by the nature of the project and a small scale. Like so many fine buildings it seems, when actually visited, much smaller than is suggested by the photograph.

26 ALVAR AALTO, Rautatalo (offices of the Steel Federation), Helsinki 1954. In many respects an unusual building for business premises located in a central position. The elegant curtain wall façade blends well with the neighbouring bank (designed by Eliel Saarinen, 1921) and the other commercial buildings in the street. On the first floor, away from the noise of the street, is the Marble Hall in which ceiling lights similar to those in the Viipuri library (cf. 8) are used with great effect.

27 ALVAR AALTO, House of Culture, Helsinki 1958. The building, which was sponsored by the Finnish Communist Party, is a solution to the problem of limited space. It is divided into a concert hall and an administrative wing. The concert hall is an asymmetrical amphiteatre. Its accoustically excellent shape is reflected in the muscular curves of the building's exterior.

28 VILJO REVELL & OSMO SIPARI, Meilahti Primary School, Helsinki 1952. The building is designed to gain maximum advantage of natural light. The curving shape is not typical of Revell's severe rationalism and in this particular case is intended to provide shelter for the playground.

29 KAIJA and HEIKKI SIREN, Studio Theatre, Helsinki 1954, an extension to the National Theatre (1902). Its interior layout is reflected clearly in the façade: the auditorium and the stage tower appear as enclosed parts while the foyer, offices and rehearsal room open onto the neighbouring park. The façade is of dark clinker.

30 VILJO REVELL & KEIJO PETÄJÄ, The Industrial Centre, Helsinki 1952. One of the occasional examples during the 1950's of Le Corbusier's influence. The basic layout of this commercial and

1 Selim A. Lindqvist 1908/1913

2 Martti Välikangas 1920-5

3 Alvar Aalto 1925

4 Sigurd Frosterus 1916/1924-30

5　Oiva Kallio 1930

6 Alvar Aalto 1929

7 Alvar Aalto 1929-33

8a & b

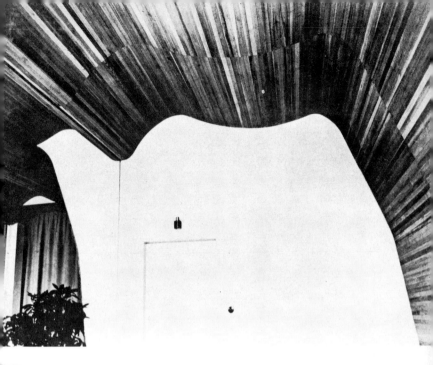

8c   Alvar Aalto 1927/1930-5

9   Alvar Aalto 1938

10   Alvar Aalto 1939

11   Alvar Aalto 1938

12   Alvar Aalto 1938

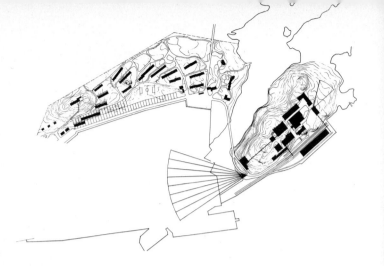

13a

13b

Alvar Aalto 1936-9/1954

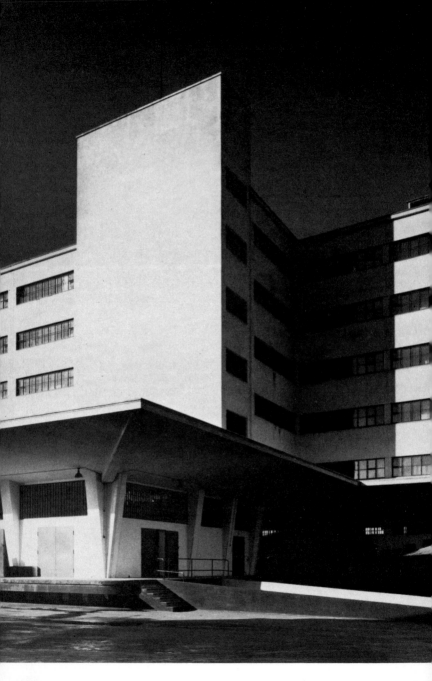

14 Erkki Huttunen 1937

15 Kokko, Revell, Riihimäki 1935

16 Pauli E. Blomstedt 1935

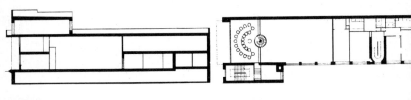

17a & b

7c Pauli E. Blomstedt 1935

18   Hilding Ekelund & Martti Välikangas 1940

19   Yrjö Lindegren & Toivo Jäntti

Gunnar Taucher 1937

21   Erik Bryggman 1949

Aulis Blomstedt 1946

23a, b & c   Yrjö Lindegren 1951

Aulis Blomstedt 1951

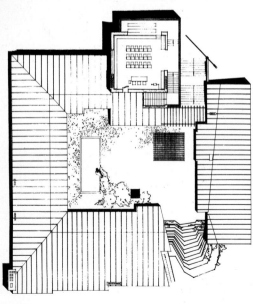

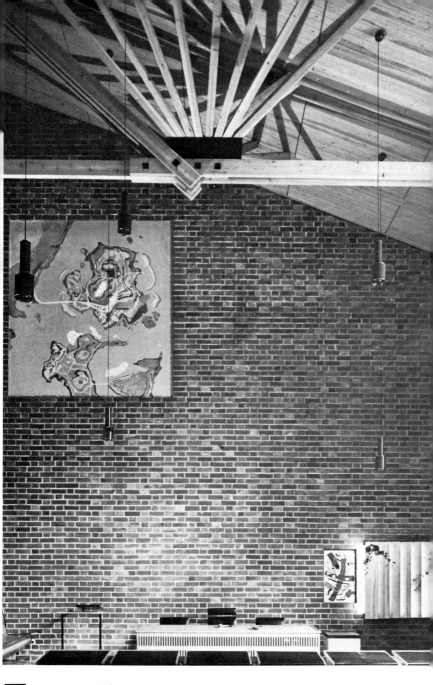

25c Alvar Aalto 1952

26a

26b Alvar Aalto 1954

27a

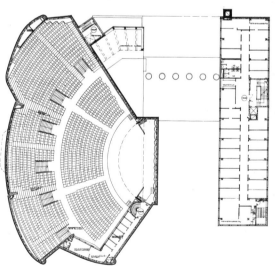

27b & c   Alvar Aalto 1958

28 Viljo Revell & Osmo Sipari 1952

29 Kaija & Heikki Siren 1954

30 Viljo Revell & Keijo Petäjä 1952

31 Alvar Aalto 1956

32a

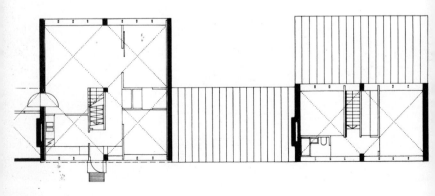

32b Aulis Blomstedt 1954

33 Aulis Blomstedt 1954

34   Viljo Revell 1958

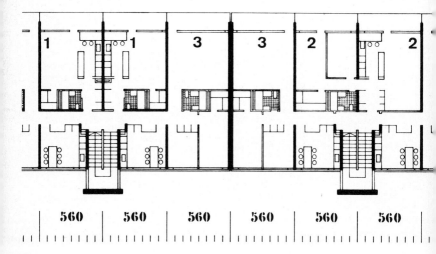

| 1 | 1 | 3 | 3 | 2 | 2 |

| 560 | 560 | 560 | 560 | 560 | 560 |

35a

35b Aulis Blomstedt 1965

36 Kaija & Heikki Siren 1955

37 Kaija & Heikki Siren 1959

38a

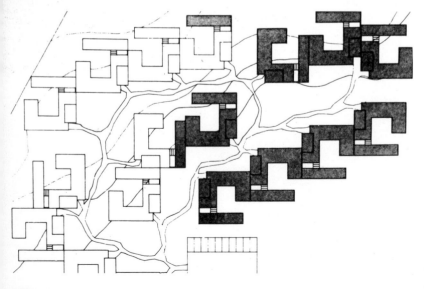

38b Pentti Ahola 1965

39a

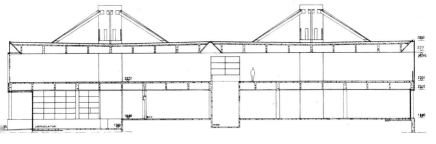

39b　Aarno Ruusuvuori 1964

40a

40b Aarno Ruusuvuori 1965

41 Aarno Ruusuvuori 1964

Kaija & Heikki Siren 1952

43a & b Kaija & Heikki Siren 1957

44   Alvar Aalto 1964

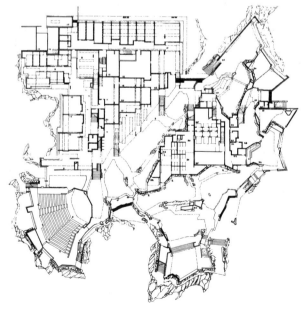

45a & b Reima Pietilä & Raili Paatelainen 1966

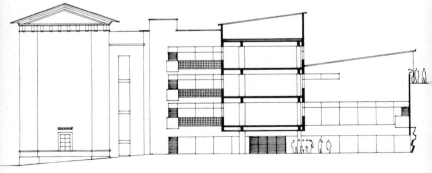

46a & b Aulis Blomstedt 1959

47 Erkki Kairamo & Jorma Pankakoski 1968

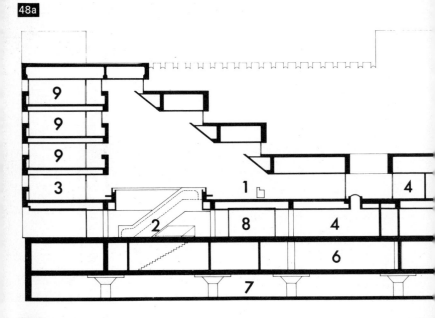

Viljo Revell 1964

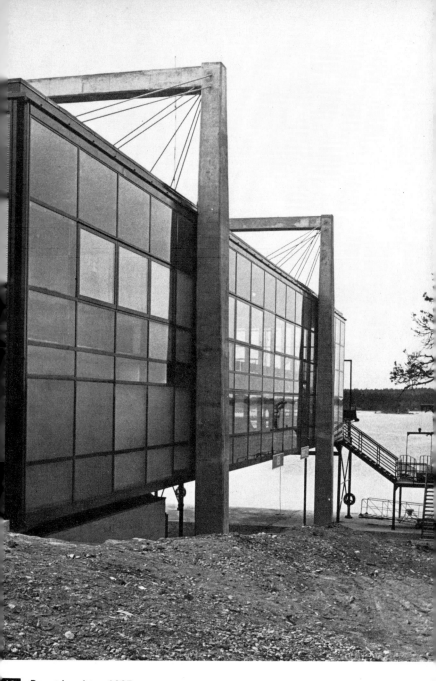

49 Bengt Lundsten 1965

50a & b Alvar Aalto 1961/1964

51a & b Timo Penttilä 1967

52 Pekka Pitkänen 1966

53 Osmo Sipari 1964

54a & b   Reima Pietilä & Raili Paatelainen 1966

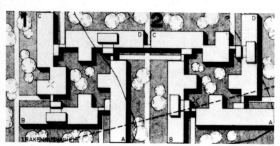

55a & b Jan Söderlund & Erkki Valovirta 1969

56a & b Kråkström, Mikkola, Pallasmaa 1967

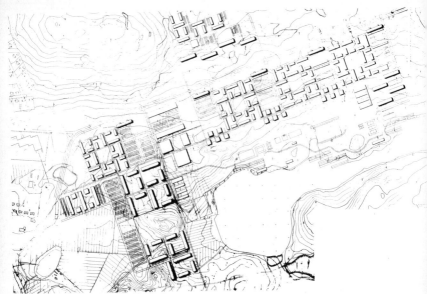

57a & b Bengt Lundsten 1968

58a & b Aarno Ruusuvuori 1967

59a & b   Kirmo Mikkola 1968

Ilkka Salo 1966

61a & b Kirmo Mikkola & Juhani Pallasmaa 1966

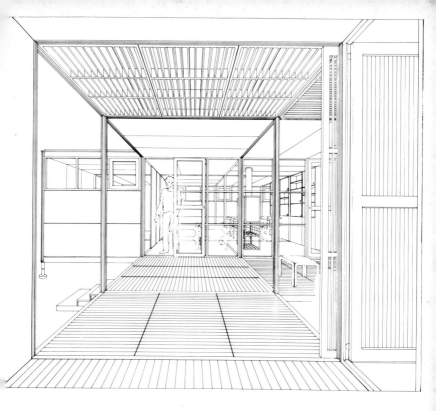

62a & b   Gullichsen, Pallasmaa, Paloheimo 1969

Aarno Ruusuvuori 1968

hotel building is H-shaped. The central part houses lifts, stair halls and other installations. The façade is extremely simple and beautifully proportioned.

31 ALVAR AALTO, National Pensions Institute, Helsinki 1956. A large office block occupying a restricted triangular site. Aalto divided the building into several parts which enclose a raised courtyard.

32 AULIS BLOMSTEDT, Ketjutalo, Tapiola 1954. The area around the Ketjutalo is an example of one of the best environments in the first stage of the development of Tapiola, Helsinki's satellite town. The Ketjutalo is a group of semi-detached dwellings arranged to form a sheltered courtyard between each pair.

33 AULIS BLOMSTEDT, Kolmirinne block of flats, Tapiola 1954. Adjacent to the Ketjutalo with which it forms a closed group. Both projects are similar in shape and constructed from similar materials.

34 VILJO REVELL, Flats in Kaskenkaataja Road, Tapiola 1958. The need for heat insulation, so essential in the Finnish climate, explains why the load-bearing reinforced concrete frame is not generally visible. Revell solves this problem by incorporating balconies in his façade which thus do away with the need for insulation.

35 AULIS BLOMSTEDT, Allakka and Kaskenkaataja flats, Tapiola 1965. The basic layout is the same as in Blomstedt's earlier works although the architectural style is simpler and more abstract.

36 KAIJA & HEIKKI SIREN, Terrace houses in Kontio Road, Tapiola 1955. Unpretentious two-storied terrace houses with a façade constructed from prefabricated wooden parts. The area, set among woods, is one of the most pleasant in Tapiola.

37 KAIJA & HEIKKI SIREN, Otsonpesä terrace houses, Tapiola 1959. A terrace of five units which, compared to 36, is coldly classical.

38 PENTTI AHOLA, Hakalehto atrium houses, Tapiola 1960. Each dwelling almost entirely encloses a small courtyard onto which most of the windows open. This inward-looking structure is especially suited to high density development.

39 AARNO RUUSUVUORI, Weilin & Göös printing works, Tapiola 1964. The method of siting the supporting columns in the printing hall affords maximum space and flexibility for machinery. The roof is divided into 'mushrooms', 26×26m in size, each of which is

supported by an unusually thick column. These columns also contain the ventilation equipment. The intermediate floor is supported by columns of normal thickness.

40 AARNO RUUSUVUORI, Tapiola Church, 1965. The overall shape of the church forms a neutral cube. Attention is mainly attracted by the fine detail, the result of much painstaking work by Ruusuvuori and his assistants.

41 AARNO RUUSUVUORI, Huutoniemi Church, Vaasa 1964. Ruusuvuori is the most uncompromisingly 'brutal' of Finnish architects. He displays an unfailingly elegant subtlety in his deliberate use of simple, coarse materials such as concrete and Leca blocks.

42
&
43 KAIJA & HEIKKI SIREN, Students' village, Otaniemi: restaurant 1952, chapel 1957. The competition for a plan to develop the Institute of Technology's site at Otaniemi was won in 1949 by Alvar Aalto with designs for a student village. The development was realised, however, by Kaija and Heikki Siren. The most sensitive expression of this uniform brick and wood architecture is the chapel, whose glass altar-wall opens out to a wooded landscape.

44 ALVAR AALTO, Institute of Technology, main building, Otaniemi 1964. The halls form the climax of the group of buildings. The steep amphitheatre made it possible for Aalto to use a most unusual lighting system: reinforced concrete arcs, which rise like steps and form shapes similar to an upside-down L, reflect the light downwards and forwards and thus prevent dazzle.

45 REIMA PIETILÄ & RAILI PAATELAINEN (PIETILÄ), *Dipoli,* students' activity centre, Otaniemi 1966. This building is regarded by many as architectural anarchy. It is anarchist in its relationship towards formalist constructivism, yet it is also the most natural and obvious solution to the problems it had to solve. The building is intended to reflect the natural background; the ground floor corridor, for example, represents a river bed and even has rocks and boulders to heighten the effect.

46 AULIS BLOMSTEDT, Annex to the Workers' Institute, Helsinki 1959. The modern annex successfully blends with the older part of the Institute (designed by Gunnar Taucher, assisted by Pauli E. Blomstedt, 1926). The new wing containing classrooms faces in the same direction as the older building. Beneath the new wing is an entrance to a small courtyard, the other side of which is sheltered by a high rock face.

47   ERKKI KAIRAMO & JORMA PANKAKOSKI, Heating plant of the Hyrylä garrison, Hyrylä 1968. Architecture as technology, a drama of pipes and machinery between two glass walls.

48   VILJO REVELL, Kansallis-Osake Pankki [Bank], Lahti 1964. The stepped windows and the powerful galleries are distinctive features of the main banking hall situated on the first floor.

49   BENGT LUNDSTEN, Passenger pavilion, Långnäs 1965. The pavilion has a bridge-like structure: two horizontal planes suspended from steel wires attached to two concrete frames. The abstract shape of pavilion, constructed from glass and steel, contrast powerfully with the surrounding skerries.

50   ALVAR AALTO, Plans for redevelopment in central Helsinki,1961-4. Aalto's task was to produce plans for developing land in the centre of the city which hitherto had not been used to maximum advantage. The designs he submitted are for a cultural centre on the bank of Töölö Bay of which concert and congress halls will be the first to be built, and, further west, for the Kamp district which will be used to extend the City development and for improving traffic conditions. Aalto's plans are characterized by a monumentalism similar to that of the baroque square.

51   TIMO PENTTILÄ, Municipal Theatre, Helsinki 1967. The theatre, the result of an architectural competition, is a magnificent building containing both the traditional large stage and a smaller, more flexible stage. The huge mass is skilfully sited on a slope near the centre of Helsinki.

52   PEKKA PITKÄNEN, Helsingin Osake Bank, Kemiö 1966. Pitkänen has undertaken considerable research into the expressive capacity of concrete in various types of buildings. Despite the apparent coarseness of the concrete, this small provincial bank has been designed with particular care. Its expressiveness is reminiscent of Le Corbusier's later concrete buildings.

53   OSMO SIPARI, Finnish-Russian School, Helsinki 1964. The large school complex is divided into several parts, each of which can function as a separate unit: boarding school, primary school, secondary school and the assembly hall building. The various sections enclose sheltered playgrounds. The façades are of concrete sandwich-elements.

54 REIMA PIETILÄ & RAILI PAATELAINEN, Kaleva Church, Tampere
    1966. A crisis in church architecture during the 1950's, resulting
    from the incompatibility of modern architectural techniques and
    out-dated traditionalism, led finally to a series of architecturally
    bold churches. The Kaleva Church is the most 'church-like' of
    these. The vertical features evoke the feeling of a cathedral.

55 JAN SÖDERLUND & ERKKI VALOVIRTA, Students' village,
    Turku, first stage 1969. The first two blocks of a large student
    village which, when completed, will form a new part of the town
    near the University. Despite high standards (accommodation con-
    sists of single rooms each with its own shower unit) costs have
    been kept low by extensive structural simplification. Internal com-
    munication between each building is afforded by a system of
    corridors and galleries.

56 ERIK KRÅKSTRÖM, KIRMO MIKKOLA, JUHANI PALLASMAA,
    Swedish secondary school, Puotila, Helsinki 1967. Evidence of
    the influence of Mies van der Rohe. The structural distinctiveness
    is repeated in the dimensional pattern in which the dimensions and
    their multiples are repeated in both the horizontal and the vertical.
    The classrooms are situated on two floors grouped around the
    assembly hall. The combined gymnasium and auditorium are in
    a separate building.

57 BENGT LUNDSTEN, Kortepohja housing development, Jyväskylä,
    first stage 1968. The development is the result of a competition
    and indicates a return to the traditional grid layout. The two-storied
    terrace houses are sited in compact blocks which enclose a park;
    motor and pedestrian traffic are isolated from each other. The ex-
    tent of the original development plans has been considerably
    modified and only a part is actually being built.

58 AARNO RUUSUVUORI, Plans for a factory-produced prefa-
    bricated house, 1967. The result of an earlier experimental house
    in which plywood was the basic material. The walls and horizontal
    surfaces consist of precast concrete slabs of standardised di-
    mensions. The houses are especially suited to high density urban
    development.

59 KIRMO MIKKOLA, Studio houses, Järvenpää 1968. Terrace
    houses built for themselves by an architect and four artists. The
    basic layout allows considerable freedom of choice in interior
planning.

60 ILKKA SALO, Summer cottage, Naantali 1966. The cottage, enclosed on two sides, opens to the sun and environment. Areas for sleeping, etc. can be isolated by means of sliding glass doors and curtains.

61 KIRMO MIKKOLA & JUHANI PALLASMAA, Relander summer house, Muurame 1966. The most representative example of a series of experimental wooden houses. Wood is better than concrete or steel for a constructivist solution for it serves as both frame and insulation. The articulated frame of the house is reminiscent of Japanese wood architecture.

62 KRISTIAN GULLICHSEN, JUHANI PALLASMAA, EERO PALO-HEIMO, Plans for a factory-produced summer house, 1969. An example of a standardized structural system particularly suited to small houses and summer cottages. This particular system is based on a unit of 225 cm. for both horizontal and vertical dimensions. There is a wide choice of wall-, floor- and roof-elements all of which can be combined in numerous ways.

63 AARNO RUUSUVUORI, Police Station, Mikkeli 1968. The building is constructed of 'cold' reinforced concrete. The use of concrete in the cells creates a marked sacral feeling.

Biographical Notes

ALVAR AALTO, b. 1898. Professor, former member of the Academy of Finland. Main works: Office building for *Turun Sanomat* newspaper; Paimio sanatorium; Viipuri library; Sunila cellulose factory with housing area; Villa Mairea; World Exhibition pavilions in Paris and New York; MIT Seniors' dormitory (USA); Säynätsalo town hall; National pensions institute; Jyväskylä University; House of culture; Vuoksenniska church; municipal and cultural centre in Seinäjoki; Technical University in Otaniemi; Cultural centre and church in Wolfsburg (Germany); Helsinki centre project; Rovaniemi library and centre project; many home and office buildings.

PENTTI AHOLA, b. 1919. Town plans; Siltamäki housing area in Helsinki; atrium houses in Tapiola and Tampere.

WOLDEMAR BAECKMAN, b. 1911. Office buildings in Helsinki; factory in Kirkonummi; Sibelius museum and other buildings for the Swedish Academy in Turku.

AULIS BLOMSTEDT, b. 1906. Professor. Main works: Workers' Institute in Helsinki; apartment houses in Helsinki and Turku; various types of houses in Tapiola; theoretical studies.

PAULI E. BLOMSTEDT, 1900-1935. Brother of Aulis Blomstedt. Main works: bank buildings in Helsinki and Kotka; interiors for alcohol industry; Kannonkoski church; Pohjanhovi hotel in Rovaniemi.

ERIK BRYGGMAN, 1891-1955. Professor. Main works: exhibition in Turku (together with Alvar Aalto); funeral chapels in Parainen and Turku; Vierumäki Sports' Institute; Book Tower and other university and students' buildings in Turku; apartment houses, hotels and office buildings in Turku.

HILDING EKELUND, b. 1893. Professor. Main works: art exhibition hall in Helsinki (together with Jarl Eklund); Olympic Village in Helsinki (together with Mattti Välikangas); velodrome and boat racing stadium, Töölö church in Helsinki; power station, apartment houses and schools.

SIGURD FROSTERUS, 1876-1956. Rationalist theories and polemic at the beginning of the century. Main works: apartment houses in Helsinki; Vanaja mansion; Stockmann's department store in Helsinki; power stations.

KRISTIAN GULLICHSEN, b. 1932. Small houses; has taken part together with Juhani Pallasmaa in developing systems for element-built apartment houses and wooden weekend-houses.

ERKKI HUTTUNEN. 1901-1956. Main works: industrial buildings for alcohol industry and SOK cooperative concern; Nakkila church; City hall in Kotka.

TOIVO JÄNTTI, b. 1900. See Yrjö *Lindegren*.

ERKKI KAIRAMO, b. 1936. Hyrylä garrison heating plant (together with Jorma Pankakoski); has taken part in the extension project for Tapiola centre and a project for the Helsinki shore-line; small houses.

OIVA KALLIO, 1884-1964. Main works: churches; Imatra power station (together with his brother Kauno S.Kallio); Pohja Insurance Company in Helsinki; apartment houses; office buildings.

NIILO KOKKO, b. 1907. See Viljo *Revell*.

ERIK KRÅKSTRÖM, b. 1919. Town plans; Lähderanta housing area; schools (some together with Ahti Korhonen); Puotila secondary school (together with Kirmo Mikkola and Juhani Pallasmaa); Helsinki Centre
project (1954 together with Yrjö Lindegren).

YRJÖ LINDEGREN, 1900-1952. Main works: hospital in Pielisjärvi; Olympic stadium in Helsinki (together with Toivo Jäntti); factories, schools; Snake house apartments in Helsinki; office buildings; plan for Helsinki centre (together with Erik Kråkström).

SELIM A. LINDQVIST, 1867-1939. Main works: office and apartment buildings in Helsinki; private houses; Town hall and water tower in Mikkeli; buildings for Helsinki city; Suvilahti power staton; distributing stations; buildings for the tramways.

BENGT LUNDSTEN, b. 1928. Professor. Main works: passenger pavilion at Långnäs; housing areas Kortepohja in Jyväskylä and Vaarala in Helsinki.

KIRMO MIKKOLA, b. 1934. Master plan and centre plan for Järvenpää (together with André Schütz); Hyrylä parish centre and small houses (mainly together with Juhani Pallasmaa); extension of Tapiola centre (together with Erkki Juutilainen, Erkki Kairamo, Juhani Pallasmaa).

RAILI PAATELAINEN (PIETILÄ) b. 1926. Works together with Reima Pietilä.

JUHANI PALLASMAA, b. 1936. See Kristian *Gullichsen*, Erik *Kråkström* and Kirmo *Mikkola*.

JORMA PANKAKOSKI, b. 1929. Garrison buildings; Hyrylä heating plant (together with Erikki Kairamo).

TIMO PENTTILÄ, b. 1931. Workers' institute and trade school in Tampere (together with Kari Virta); Ratina stadium in Tampere; Helsinki city theatre; apartment houses; parish centre in Karkku.

KEIJO PETÄJÄ, b. 1919. Industrial centre office building (together with Viljo Revell); Lauttasaari church in Helsinki; schools; apartment houses; administrative and parish centres in Ulmajoki and Turenki.

REIMA PIETILÄ, b. 1923. Kaleva church in Tampere; Dipoli students' club house in Otaniemi; Suvikumpu apartment houses in Tapiola; project for Kuwait centre (together with Raili Paatelainen).

PEKKA PITKÄNEN, b. 1927. Main works: bank building in Kemiö: office building in Turku; students' apartment houses; crematorium in Turku.

VILJO REVELL, 1910-1964. Main works: Glass Palace in Helsinki (together with Niilo Kokko and Heimo Riihimäki); Industrial centre in Helsinki (together with Keijo Petäjä); housing areas in Helsinki and Vaasa; Kudeneule textile factory in Hanko; other factories; bank buildings in Turku and Lahti; office and business blocks in Helsinki and Vaasa; Toronto city hall (competition together with Heikki Castrén, Bengt Lundsten, Seppo Valjus; realization together with J. B. Parkin & Ass.).

HEIMO RIIHIMÄKI, b. 1907. See Viljo *Revell*.

AARNO RUUSUVUORI, b. 1925. Professor. Main works: Huutoniemi church in Vaasa; churches in Hyvinkää and Tapiola; printing factory in Tapiola; police house in Mikkeli; renewal of City hall and other old buildings in Helsinki; apartment houses.

ILKKA SALO, b. 1934. Small houses; interiors.

OSMO SIPARI, b. 1922. Main works: Finnish-Russian school in Helsinki; many other schools; apartment houses; funeral chapel in Kemi.

HEIKKI SIREN, b. 1918. Main works: technical students' village in Otaniemi (housing, restaurant, chapel); studio theatre in Helsinki; Orivesi church; schools in Helsinki, Hamina and Kemi; apartment houses and office buildings (together with Kaija Siren).

KAIJA SIREN, b. 1920, works together with Heikki Siren.

JAN SÖDERLUND, b. 1937. Small houses; students' village in Turku (together with Erkki Valovirta).

GUNNAR TAUCHER, 1886-1941. City architect in Helsinki. Main works: Workers' Institute in Helsinki; municipal apartment houses; schools; fire station; warehouse.

ERKKI VALOVIRTA, b. 1942. See Jan *Söderlund*.

MARTTI VÄLIKANGAS, b. 1893. Main works: Käpylä garden city in Helsinki; apartment houses; office buildings.